NELSON ESSENTIAL GEOGRAPHY SKILLS

RUTH **NAUMANN**
MARYELLEN **DAVIDSON**
ELEANOR **RICHARDS**

SECOND EDITION

Nelson Essential Geography Skills
2nd Edition
Eleanor Richards
Ruth Naumann
Maryellen Davidson

Publishing editors: Tanya Wasylewski and Michael Spurr
Project editor: Aynslie Harper
Editor: Sylvia Marson
Text designer: Astred Hicks
Cover designer: Ruth O'Connor
Permissions researcher: Kaitlin Jordan
Production controller: Julie McArthur
Typeset by: Q2A Media

ISBN 978 0 17 036707 3

Cengage Learning Australia
Level 7, 80 Dorcas Street
South Melbourne, Victoria Australia 3205

Cengage Learning New Zealand
Unit 4B Rosedale Office Park
331 Rosedale Road, Albany, North Shore 0632, NZ

For learning solutions, visit cengage.com.au

Printed in Malaysia by Papercraft.
13 14 15 25 24

CONTENTS

UNIT 1
GLOSSARY

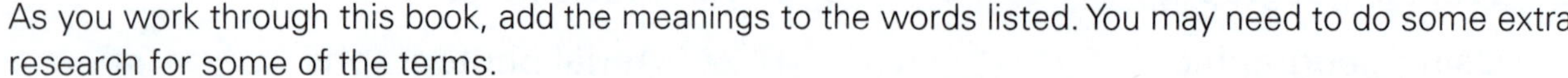

As you work through this book, add the meanings to the words listed. You may need to do some extra research for some of the terms.

absolute distance ______________________

aerial photograph ______________________

anticyclone ______________________

area references ______________________

asylum seeker ______________________

atmosphere ______________________

axis ______________________

BALTS ______________________

bar graph ______________________

biosphere ______________________

birth rate ______________________

BOLTSS ______________________

cardinal points ______________________

change ______________________

choropleth ______________________

climate ______________________

climate change ______________________

climograph ______________________

clustered pattern ______________________

cold front ______________________

compass ______________________

compass rose ______________________

concave slope ______________________

contemporary issue ______________________

contour line ______________________

convex slope ______________________

cross-section ______________________

data ______________________

death rate ______________________

demographic transition model ______________________

desalination ______________________

depression (of relief) ______________________

depression (of weather) ______________________

direction ______________________

dispersed pattern ______________________

distance ______________________

distribution ______________________

drought ______________________

earthquake ______________________

easting ______________________

ecological footprint ______________________

ELDC ______________________

El Niño ______________________

environment ______________________

Equator ______________________

evapotranspiration ______________________

exceptions (outliers) ______________________

feedback ______________________

field sketch ______________________

field work ______________________

flood ______________________

flow chart ______________________

GEED ______________________

geographer ______________________

geographic issue ______________________

geography ______________________

global scale ______________________

grid references ______________________

hemisphere ______________________

hill ______________________

historical issue ______________________

human features ______________________

hydrosphere ______________________

inputs ______________________

interconnection ______________________

international scale ______________________

ISBN 9780170367073

isobar ______

landforms ______

latitude ______

life expectancy ______

line of best fit ______

lithosphere ______

linear pattern ______

line graph ______

local scale ______

location ______

logging ______

longitude ______

map ______

maternal health ______

megacities ______

migrants ______

mind map ______

national scale ______

natural features ______

natural increase ______

northing ______

oblique angle view ______

occluded front ______

outputs ______

pass ______

percentage ______

percentage bar graph ______

pie graph ______

place ______

plateau ______

population pyramid ______

poverty cycle ______

PQE ______

precis map ______

precis sketch ______

prime meridian (Greenwich meridian) ______

processes ______

pull factors ______

push factors ______

questionnaire ______

random pattern ______

recycling ______

regional scale ______

relationship ______

relative distance ______

relief ______

resource ______

ridge ______

salinity ______

scale ______

scatter graph ______

space ______

spatial ______

SPICESS ______

spur ______

star diagram ______

stationary front ______

survey ______

surveyor ______

sustainability ______

system diagram ______

topographic map ______

topography ______

tornado ______

total fertility rate ______

tropical cyclone ______

uniform slope ______

urbanisation ______

valley ______

variable ______

Venn diagram ______

vertical angle view ______

volcano ______

warm front ______

water cycle ______

weather ______

weather map ______

whaling ______

winds ______

ISBN 9780170367073

UNIT 2

WHAT IS GEOGRAPHY?

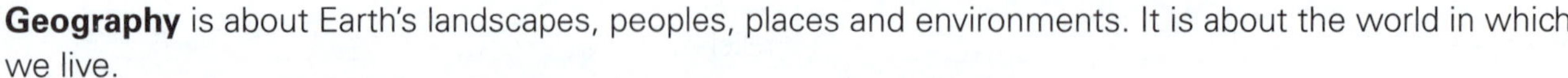

Geography is about Earth's landscapes, peoples, places and environments. It is about the world in which we live.

The word comes from the Greek words *geo*, meaning 'the earth', and *graphy*, meaning 'to draw, write, represent, record or describe something'.

A **geographer** is a person who studies or writes about geography.

Geography is about the past, the present and the future; it helps you make choices and understand the impact of those choices.

Today, the core of Geography in Australian schools is expressed through its key concepts, which are:

SPICESS

Space – Where places are located and how features are spread out across the Earth's surface. This is the concept that the majority of people would relate to as Geography. Where are the different countries and places in the world? How are features on the Earth's surface spread out? Ask your parents what they studied in Geography – this is probably the only one of the SPICESS that they can remember studying in detail.

Place – How an area is identified and what it means to the people who live there. A good example of 'place' is to think about your school. What makes it special? What makes it part of the community? Who are the people who go to your school and how do you recognise them?

Interconnections – How things are connected with each other and the consequences of this. Possibly the hardest of all the concepts in Geography to understand. Think about a surfer or a skier. How do they use the wave or the slope to get from the sea to the beach or from the top of a hill to the bottom? What happens if the wave is too small or the slope of the hill is too steep?

Change – How a situation has changed over time (change over time) or where things have moved from and to (change over space). Of all the aspects that make up Geography, this is probably the easiest to understand. We can see change and we can describe it. How have you changed since you started school?

Environment – The physical and biological world around us that supports and makes our lives better. An example of a human environment might be your bedroom. Go to Google Images and search 'where children sleep' to see the very different environments of children from around the world.

Sustainability – How we can use and manage our world so that future generations have the same resources available to them. Children's picture story books that discuss the environment and how we use it can provide good examples of sustainability and what it means in simple terms. Dr Seuss' *The Lorax* or Graeme Base's *Uno's Garden* are good examples. In small groups reread these stories (or any others you can think of) and discuss with members of the group what the story told you about sustainability.

Scale – The level at which we look at issues. For example, do these issues only affect people in one area or people all over the world? Two examples of issues of different scale would be the introduction of bike paths in your local area (local scale) and the United Nations Conference on Climate Change in December 2015 (global scale).

ISBN 9780170367073

All the physical aspects of Geography fit into one of the following spheres.

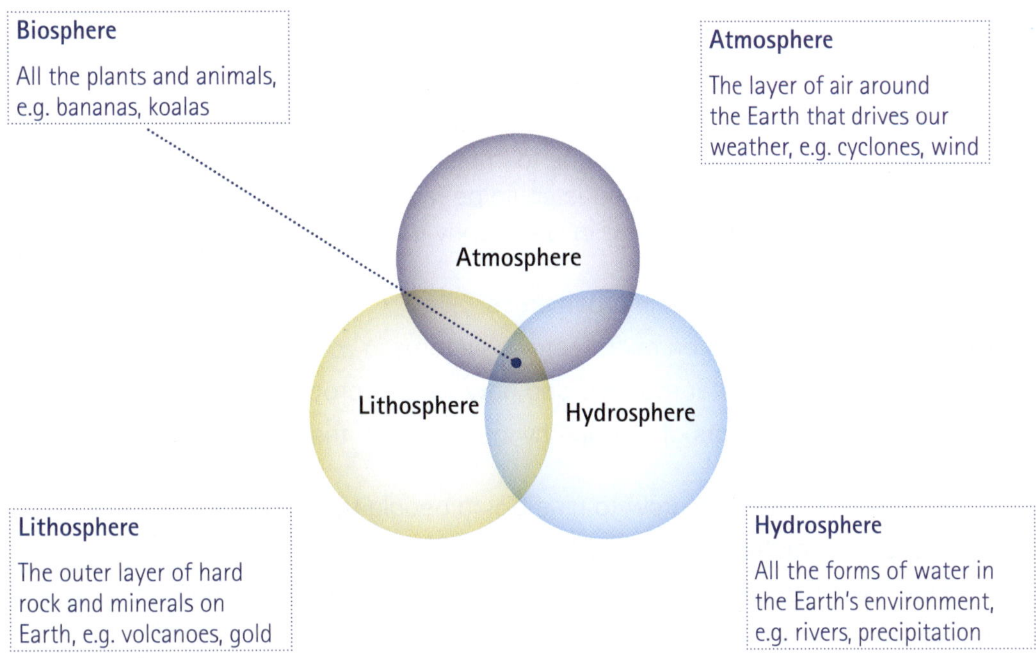

1 For the issues listed below, state whether they are of local, national, international or global scale.

Asylum seekers ______________________

Salinity in the Murray-Darling Basin ______________________

Your school introduces a new uniform ______________________

Climate change ______________________

2 Write each of the following items into the table under the correct geographical category.

wattle, earthquake, rain, tornado, flood, Mount Kosciuszko, crocodile, ozone layer, gold, drought, Great Barrier Reef, Sydney Harbour

Biosphere	Lithosphere	Hydrosphere	Atmosphere

UNIT 3
USING GEOGRAPHIC CONCEPTS

Many of the topics and concepts that are covered in Geography ask you to think about the current situation in a location and then to propose changes to improve the situation in the future. You will then need to consider what further problems or issues could be raised by your suggested changes.

Some different topics that you might cover in Geography that involve looking at decision making and future outcomes include the:

- problems of transport and congestion in urban areas
- impact that population growth has on rainforest ecosystems
- changes that are made to our water systems and how we can protect them.

In order to start using the concepts of Geography introduced in the previous unit, think about the following possibilities:

- the world's population continues to grow to nine billion people by 2050
- climate change alters the distribution of rainfall
- countries with low rainfall begin to run out of water and people migrate to find more water
- underground water begins to dry up because too much has been used.

GROUP ACTIVITY

Choose one of the seven topics listed above. Each person in the group completes a short oral presentation to the rest of the group using these opening sentences:

1 I am thinking of ... [the topic] ... from the point of view of ... [the viewpoint you've chosen].
2 I think ... [describe the topic from your viewpoint. Be an actor and take on the character of your viewpoint].
3 A question I have from this viewpoint is ... [ask a question from this viewpoint].

Once everyone in your group has presented a different point of view, discuss:

1 The new ideas your group has about the topic.
2 What new questions do you have?

Choose one person from your group to present the topic and the answer to the last two questions above to the rest of the class.

Three Gorges Dam, China

Yangtze River, 17 April 1987

Yangtze River, 7 November 2006

NASA Earth Observatory

ISBN 9780170367073

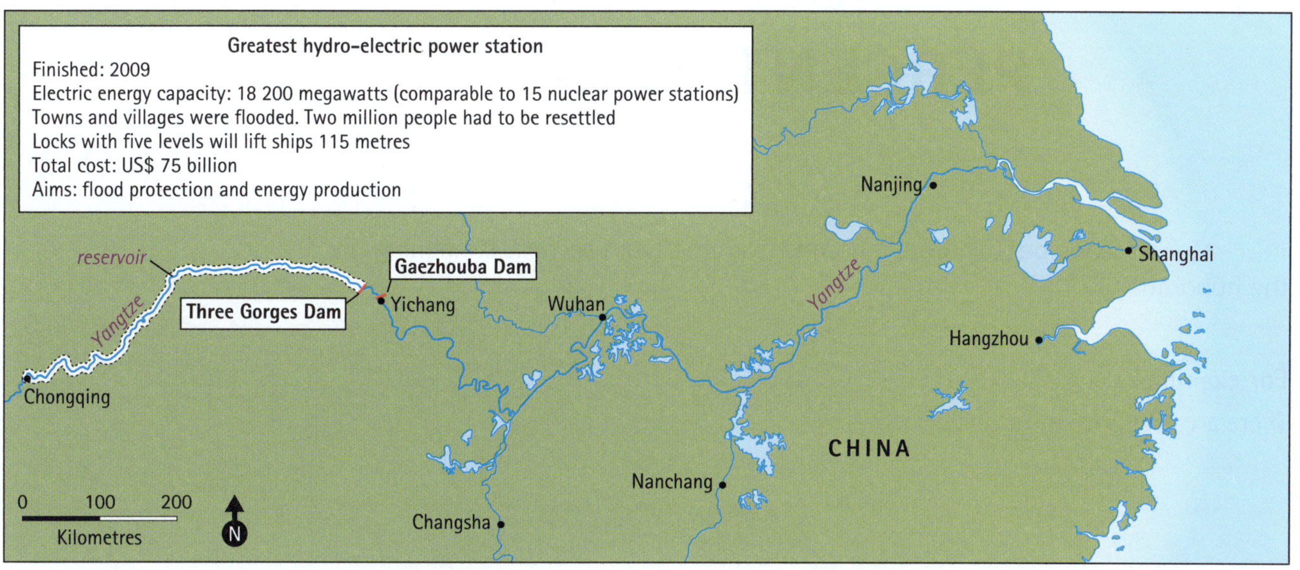

1 Use the images on the previous page and the map above to give examples of each of the seven spatial concepts. (See Unit 2 **SPICESS**)

a Describe the *space* of the Three Gorges Dam.

i What country is it located in? ______________________________

ii Where is it located in relation to other cities? ______________________________

iii Use an Internet source or an atlas to look up the latitude and longitude of the Three Gorges Dam.

____

b How would you describe the shape of the land in this *place*?

____

c What is the *interconnection* between the dam and the people?

____

d Describe the *change* in the shape of the river from 1987 to 2006.

____

e What would be the impact of this dam on the *environment*?

____

f How is this a *sustainable* way to produce energy?

____

g On what *scale* should the Three Gorges Dam project be discussed (national, international or global)?

____

ISBN 9780170367073

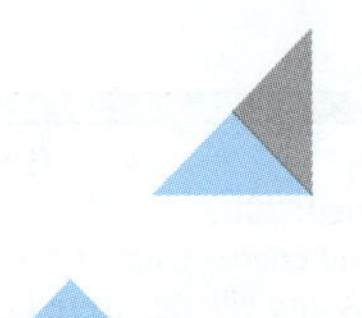

UNIT 4
PERCENTAGES

Percentage means per hundred. It comes from the Latin *per centum* meaning 'by the hundred'.

Percentage symbol = %

For example:

There are 100 ticks in the box below.

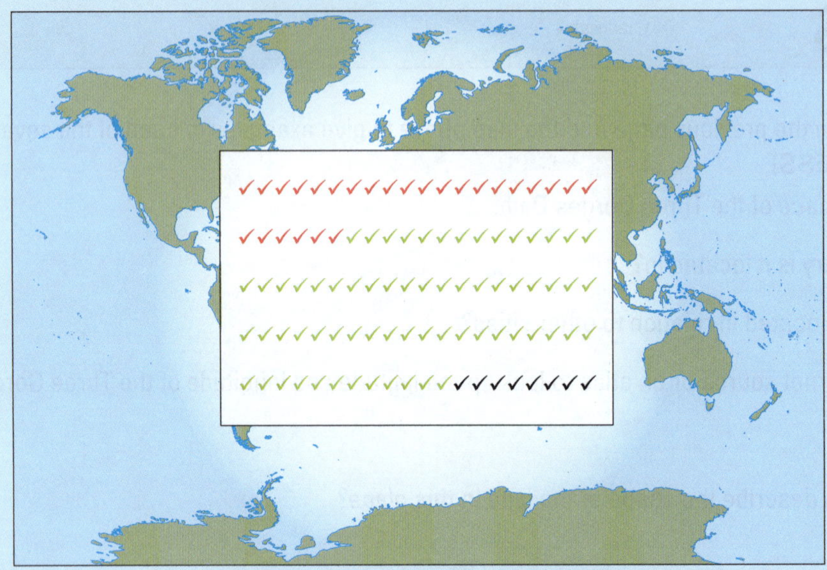

Imagine that these ticks stand for the whole population of the world. The red ticks show the people aged below 15 years. Twenty six ticks are red. This means that 26 per cent of the world's population are aged below 15 years. The black ticks are for people aged 66 years or more. There are eight black ticks. This means that 8 per cent of the world's population is older than 65. The green ticks are the rest of the population. This means that 66 ticks are left. These are the people aged between 15 and 65 and they make up 66 per cent of the world's population.

Percentages can also show fractions

For example: $\frac{1}{5} = 20\%$

$20\% + 20\% + 20\% + 20\% + 20\% = 100\%$

To change a fraction to a percentage, multiply by 100

For example:

to change $\frac{1}{5}$ to a percentage

$\frac{1}{5} \times \frac{100}{1} = \frac{100}{5}$

$= 20$

$= 20\%$

Why it's good to be able to work out percentages

- It is a skill you can use in all your subjects and for all your life.
- It helps you to perform other tasks, such as drawing graphs.
- Percentages are an easy way to show data.

ISBN 9780170367073

How to work out a percentage

Example: Australia's Aboriginal and Torres Strait Islander population in 2011.

1 New South Wales	208 476	5 Western Australia	88 270
2 Victoria	47 333	6 Tasmania	24 165
3 Queensland	188 954	7 Northern Territory	68 850
4 South Australia	37 408	8 ACT	6160

TOTAL = 669 616

Note: Because of rounding errors, the total may not always add to exactly 100%.

Example 1 $\frac{208\,476}{669\,616} \times \frac{100}{1} = 31.13\%$

Example 2 $\frac{47\,333}{669\,616} \times \frac{100}{1} = 7.07\%$

Example 3 $\frac{188\,954}{669\,616} \times \frac{100}{1} = 28.22\%$

Example 4 $\frac{37\,408}{669\,616} \times \frac{100}{1} = 5.59\%$

Example 5 $\frac{88\,270}{669\,616} \times \frac{100}{1} = 13.18\%$

Example 6 $\frac{24\,165}{669\,616} \times \frac{100}{1} = 3.61\%$

Example 7 $\frac{68\,850}{669\,616} \times \frac{100}{1} = 10.28\%$

Example 8 $\frac{6160}{669\,616} \times \frac{100}{1} = 0.92\%$

1 Change the following fractions into percentages.

a $\frac{1}{4}$ ________________

b $\frac{2}{3}$ ________________ (you will need to round the answer up)

c $\frac{1}{5}$ ________________

d $\frac{3}{5}$ ________________

2 This bar diagram represents the Aboriginal and Torres Strait Islander population of Australia in 2011. Using the information provided above, match each state to the correct percentage and write the total percentage (rounded up).

Aboriginal and Torres Strait Islander population of Australia, 2011

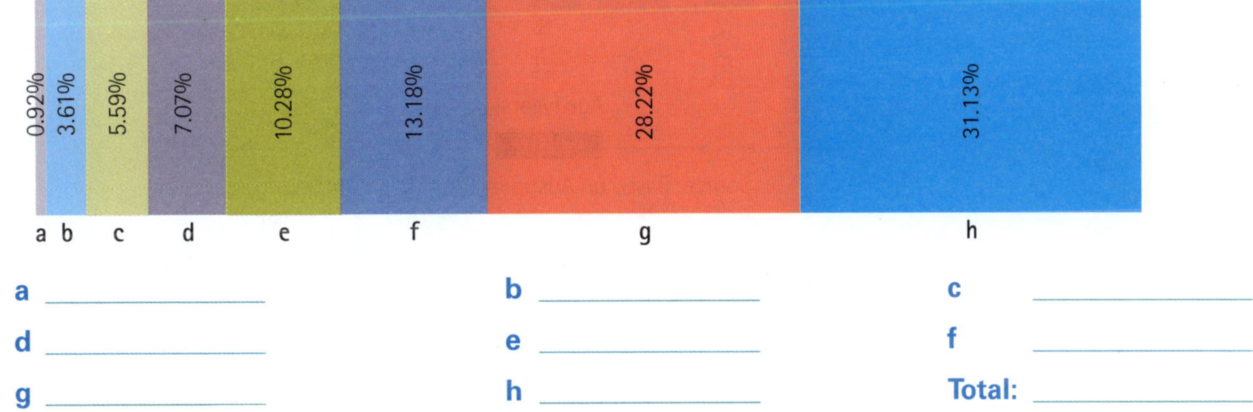

a ________ **b** ________ **c** ________

d ________ **e** ________ **f** ________

g ________ **h** ________ **Total:** ________

3 Use a calculator to work out the following percentages of age groups in the population of Aboriginal and Torres Strait Islanders in Australia in 2011 (round your answers). The total population was 669 616.

Age	Number	Percentage of population
0–14	240 620	
15–64	406 579	
65+	29 712	

Source: 3238.0.55.001 – Estimates of Aboriginal and Torres Strait Islander Australians, June 2011, Australian Bureau of Statistics.

UNIT 5
BAR GRAPHS

Graphs are a useful way to communicate information visually. They are frequently used in Geography, and other disciplines, to convey information in a way that enables relationships to be more clearly seen.

Bar graphs are one of the most common forms of graphs. They are called bar graphs because the information is represented in bars or columns. They are often used to compare information. Remember BALTS when creating bar graphs.

BALTS
Border
Axis labels and scale
Legend
Title
Source

EXAMPLE OF A BAR GRAPH

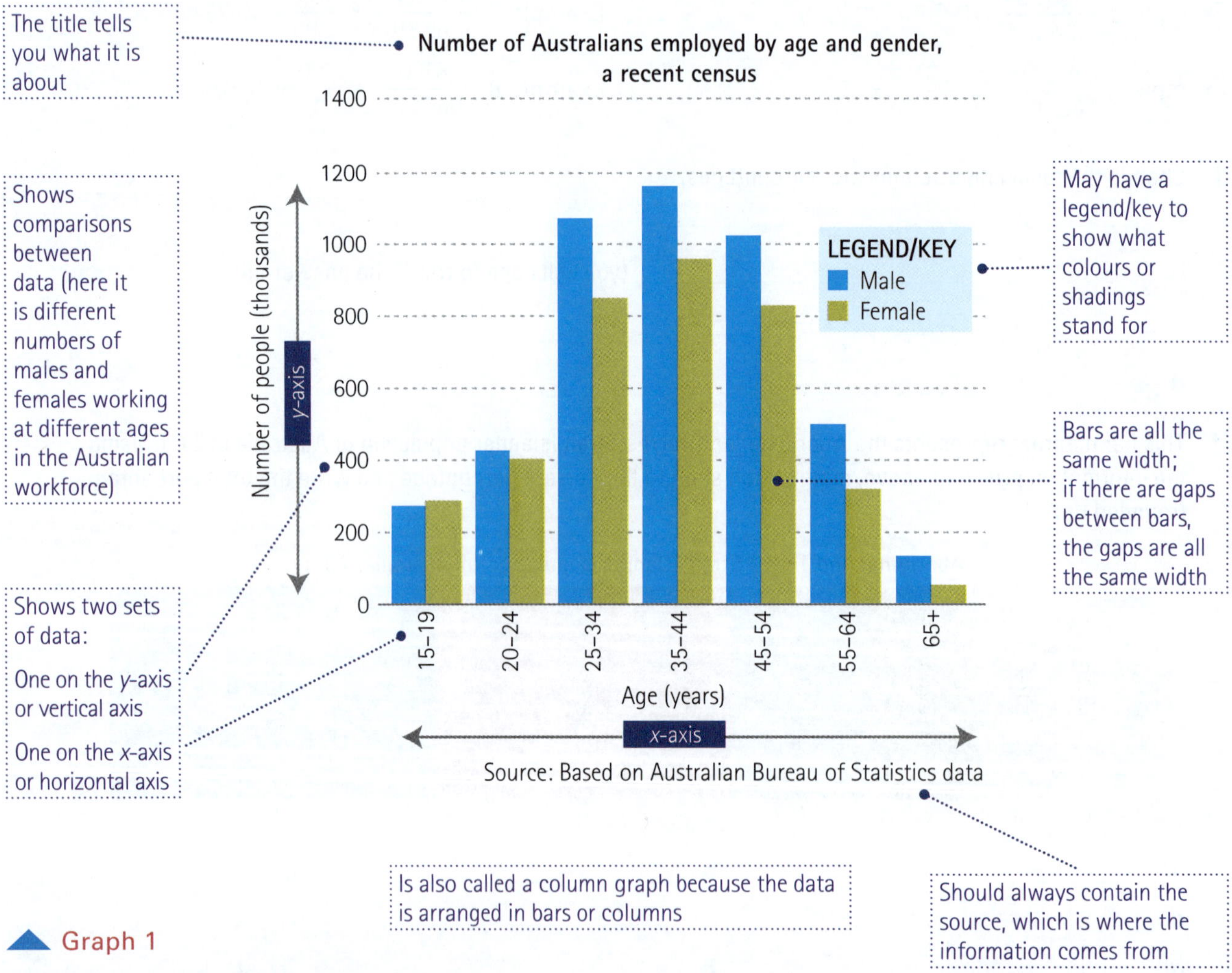

The title tells you what it is about

Number of Australians employed by age and gender, a recent census

Shows comparisons between data (here it is different numbers of males and females working at different ages in the Australian workforce)

Number of people (thousands)

y-axis

1400
1200
1000
800
600
400
200
0

LEGEND/KEY
Male
Female

May have a legend/key to show what colours or shadings stand for

Bars are all the same width; if there are gaps between bars, the gaps are all the same width

Shows two sets of data:

One on the *y*-axis or vertical axis

One on the *x*-axis or horizontal axis

15–19
20–24
25–34
35–44
45–54
55–64
65+

Age (years)

x-axis

Source: Based on Australian Bureau of Statistics data

Is also called a column graph because the data is arranged in bars or columns

Should always contain the source, which is where the information comes from

Graph 1

1 Complete the following statements about Graph 1.

a The graph has come from the ____________________________________.

b The vertical axis is also called the ____________________ axis.

c The number of people in thousands is shown on the ____________________ axis.

d The horizontal axis is also called the ____________________ axis.

e The ages are shown on the ____________________ axis.

ISBN 9780170367073

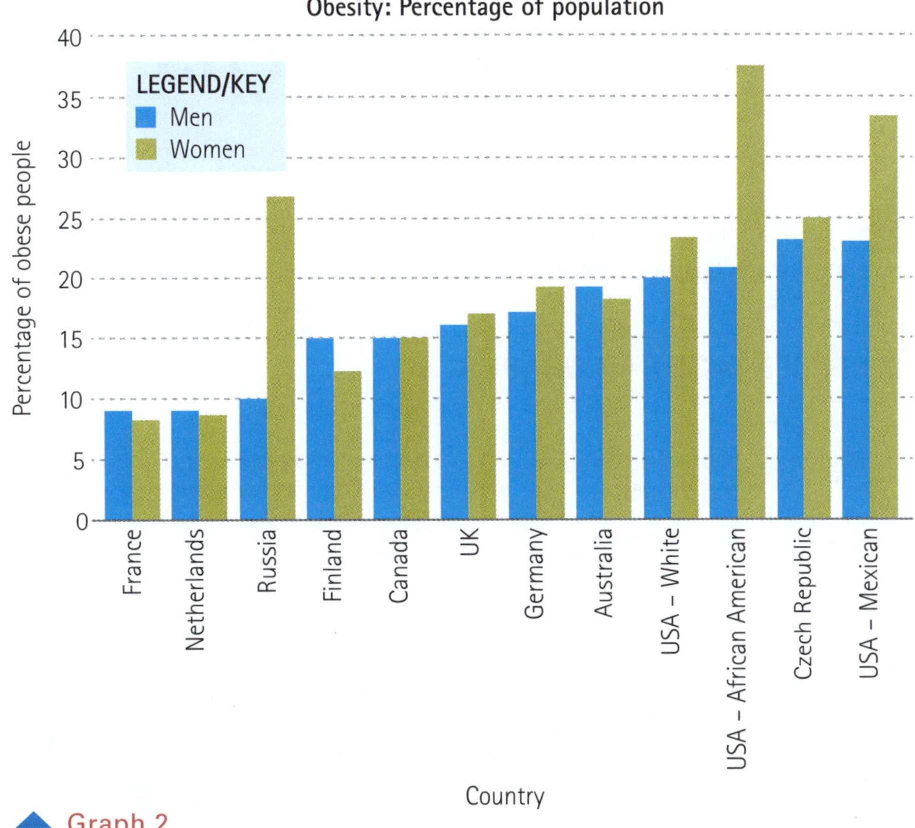

Graph 2

2 Complete the following statements about Graph 2.

a The country data is shown on the ______________________ axis.

b The percentage of obese people is shown on the ______________________ axis.

c The highest number for obesity is (percentage, gender, country) ______________________.

d The lowest number for obesity is (percentage, gender, country) ______________________.

3 Use the data from the table below to create a bar graph on the axes below. Remember: **BALTS**.

THE POPULATION OF AUSTRALIA'S LARGEST FIVE CAPITAL CITIES	
City	**Population in thousands**
Sydney	4605.9
Melbourne	4169.14
Brisbane	2146.6
Adelaide	1262.9
Perth	1832.1

Source: Based on Australian Bureau of Statistics data

5000
4500
4000
3500
3000
2500
2000
1500
1000
500
0

ISBN 9780170367073

UNIT 6
PERCENTAGE BAR GRAPHS

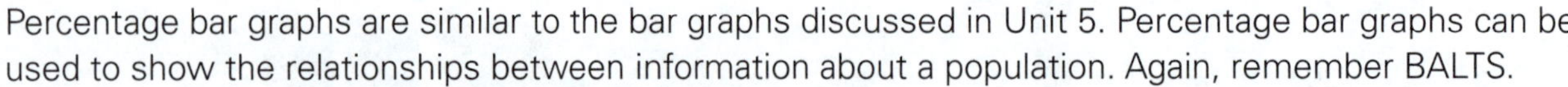

Percentage bar graphs are similar to the bar graphs discussed in Unit 5. Percentage bar graphs can be used to show the relationships between information about a population. Again, remember BALTS.

EXAMPLES OF PERCENTAGE BAR GRAPHS

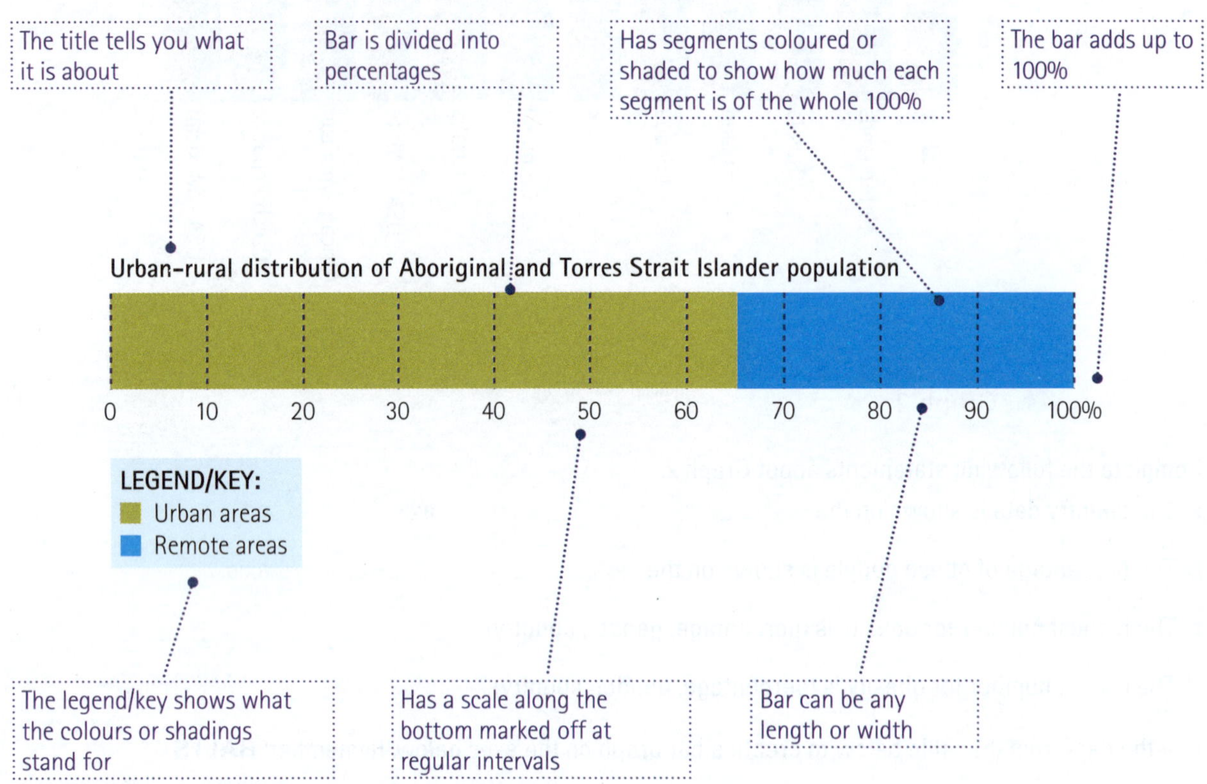

Gabbi drew this bar graph to show the percentage of Australian-born students in her school.

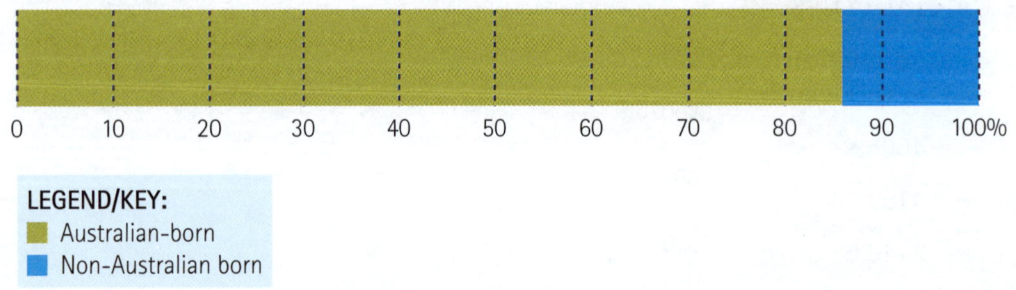

ISBN 9780170367073

1 **a** On the first example graph on page 12, what percentage of Aboriginal and Torres Strait Islander people live in urban areas? ____________________

b On Graph 1, below, use two colours to show that English is the first language for 77 per cent of the Australian population.

c On Graph 2, below, use two colours to show that Christianity is the religion of 61.1 per cent of the Australian population.

d Complete the legends for both graphs by adding the correct colours.

Graph 1

Percentage of Australians with English as their first language

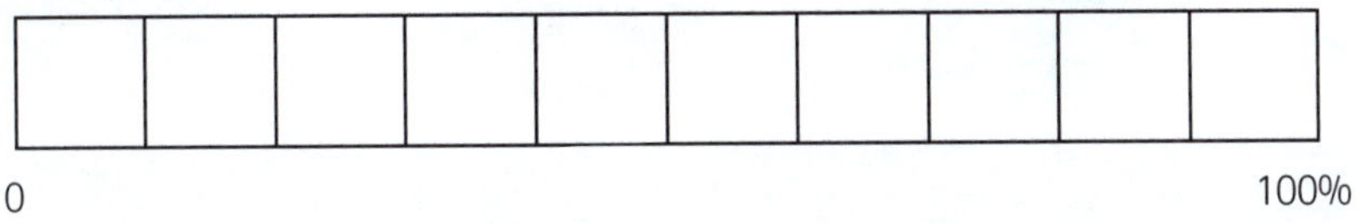

0 100%

LEGEND/KEY:
- English
- Other (e.g. Chinese, Italian)

Graph 2

Percentage of Australians whose religion is Christianity

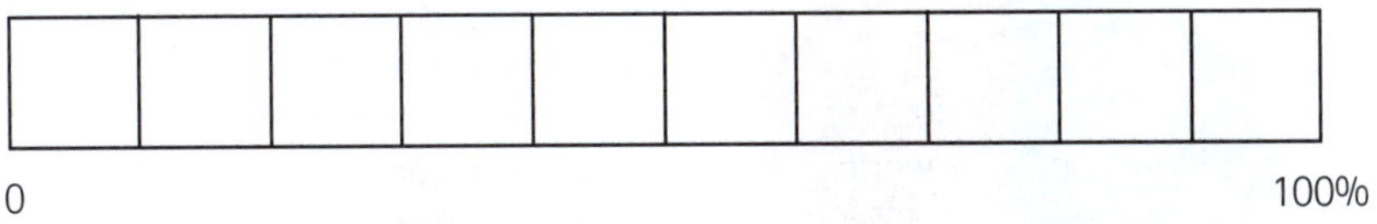

0 100%

LEGEND/KEY:
- Christian
- Non-Christian (e.g. Buddhist, Muslim)

2 Use the key to finish Rob's Year 10 class percentage bar graph. Use four different colours on your graph.

LEGEND/KEY:
- Australian-born (89%)
- European-born (3%)
- New Zealand-born (3%)
- Asian-born (5%)

Rob's Year 10 class

UNIT 7
PIE GRAPHS

A **pie graph** is circular in shape, like a pie. Pie graphs are a good way to show percentages.

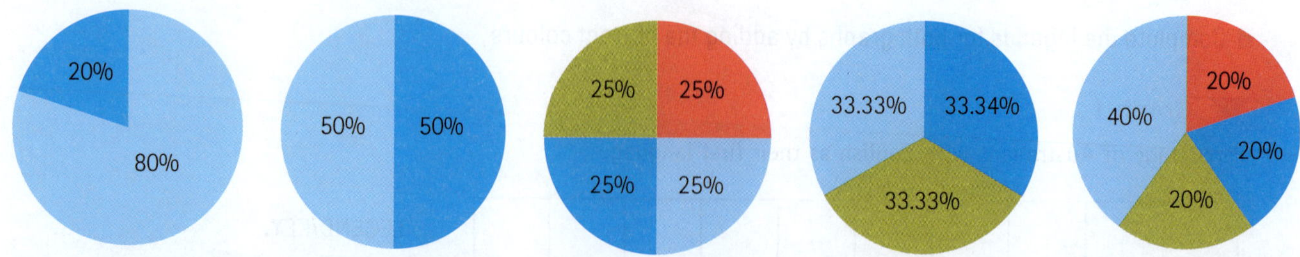

Percentages of a pie graph must add up to 100%

EXAMPLE OF A PIE GRAPH

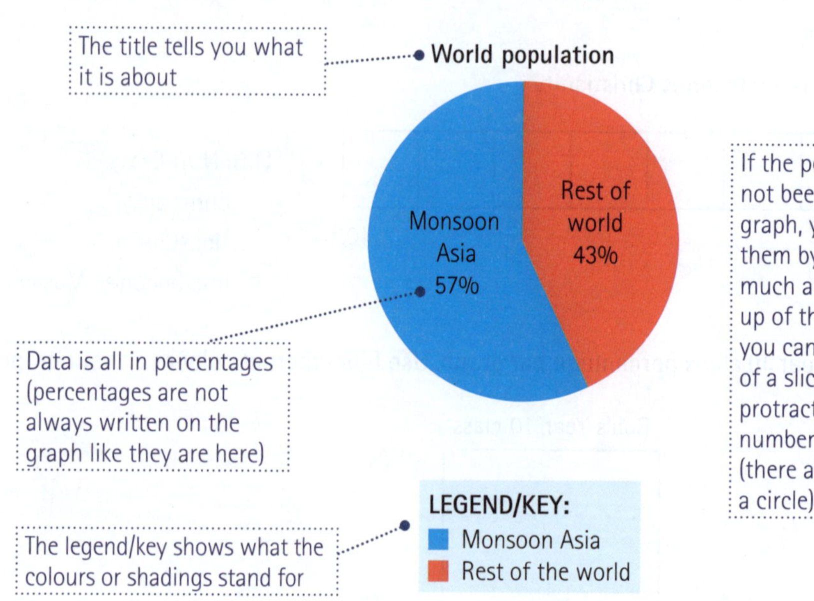

If the percentages have not been written on the graph, you can estimate them by looking at how much a slice/sector takes up of the whole circle OR you can measure the angle of a slice/sector with a protractor and divide the number of degrees by 3.6 (there are 360 degrees in a circle)

1 Use different colours on the following pie graphs and add the colours to the legends/keys.

a Ethnic percentages in Singapore

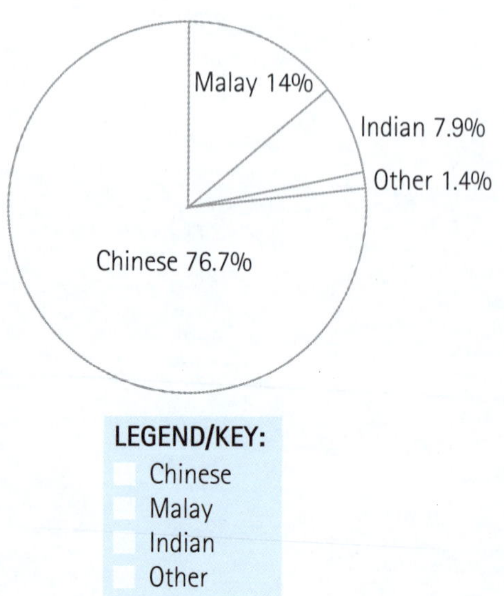

LEGEND/KEY:
- Chinese
- Malay
- Indian
- Other

b Ethnic percentages in Australia

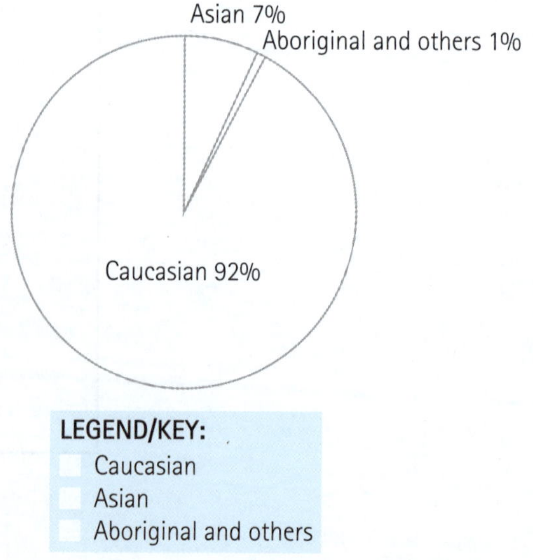

LEGEND/KEY:
- Caucasian
- Asian
- Aboriginal and others

ISBN 9780170367073

2 Write the following data into the correct slices on the graph.

Javanese 45%, Sundanese 14%, Madurese 7.5%, Coastal Malays 7.5%, Other 26%

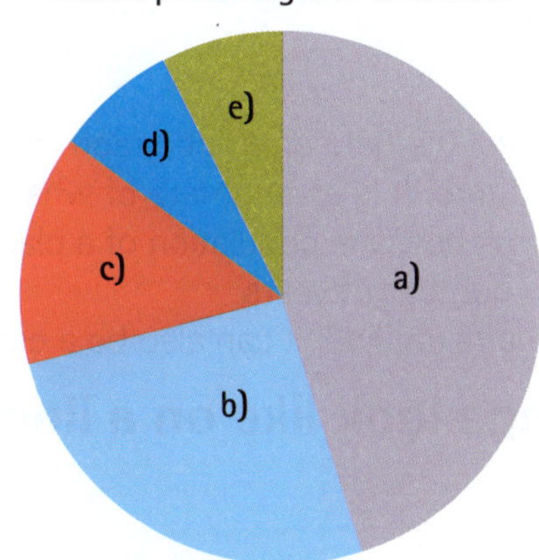

3 Use the pie graph below, which shows the percentage of migrants to Australia in each age group, to answer the following questions.

a According to the graph, what age are the majority of migrants? ______________________________

b According to the graph, at what age do the least number of migrants arrive? ______________________

Percentage of migrants to Australia in each age group

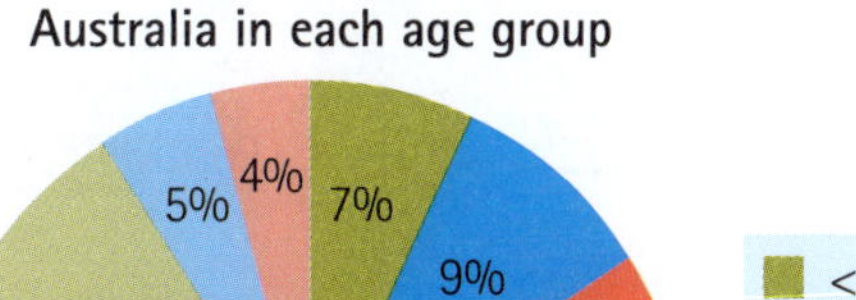

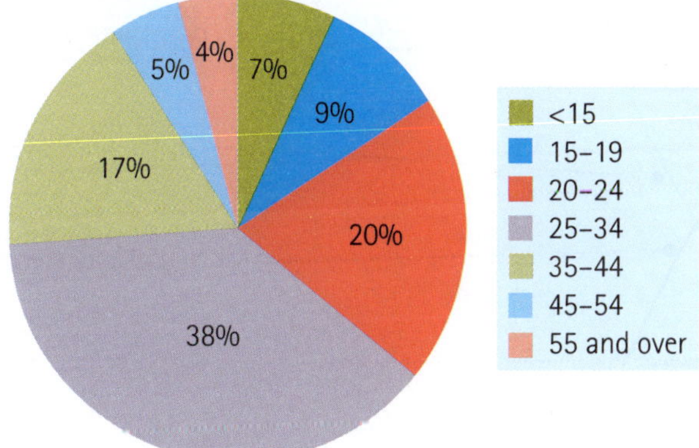

Source: Based on Australian Bureau of Statistics data

4 Use the information on population percentages, provided below, to draw your own pie chart that shows the breakdown of the population of the states and territories of Australia. Don't forget BALTS.

State	%
New South Wales	32.0
Victoria	24.9
Queensland	20.1
South Australia	7.2
Western Australia	11.0
Tasmania	2.2
Northern Territory	1.0
Australian Capital Territory	1.6

Source: ABS, Australian Demographic Statistics – 2014

UNIT 8
LINE GRAPHS

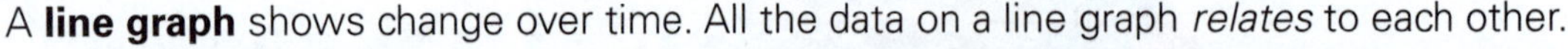

A **line graph** shows change over time. All the data on a line graph *relates* to each other.

Projected data tells you about the future. It is an estimate of what the statistician thinks will happen.

For example, a line graph might show how the population of a place has changed (increased or decreased or fluctuated) over a certain number of years.

A line graph does not need to be a straight line; it can also be a curve.

What lines showing change look like on a line graph

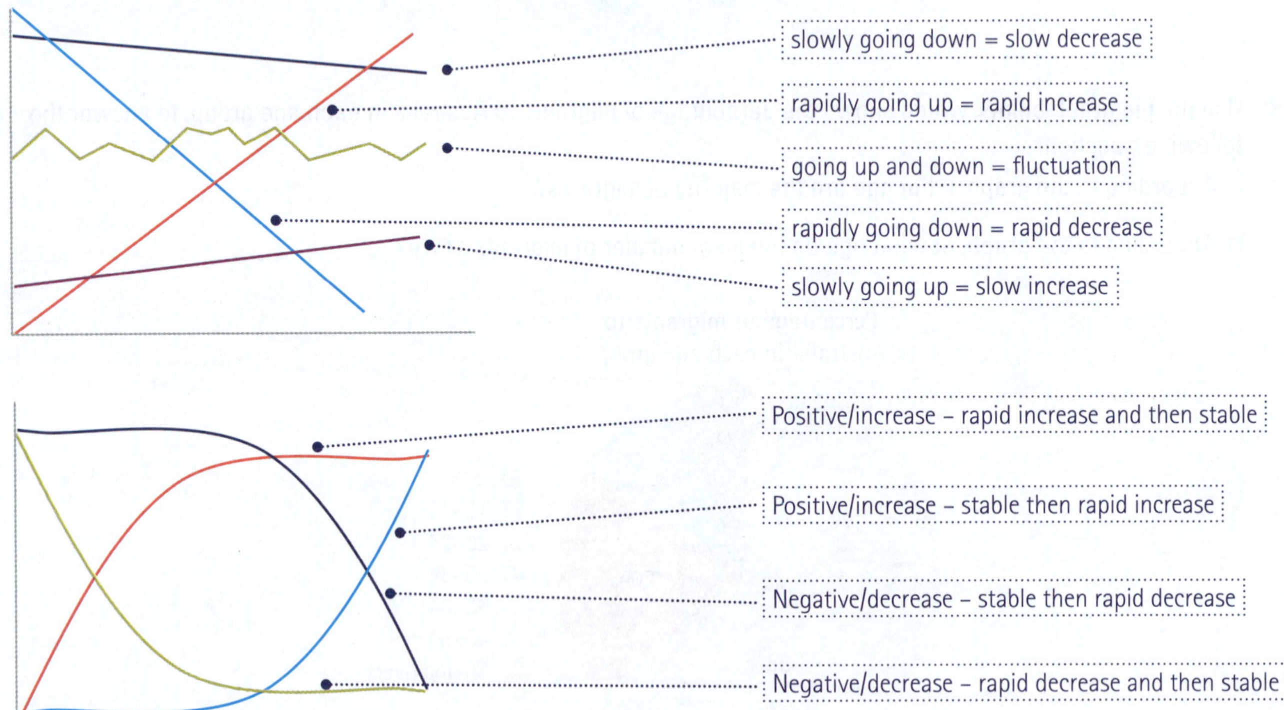

1 In the spaces provided, write the type of change shown by these graph lines.

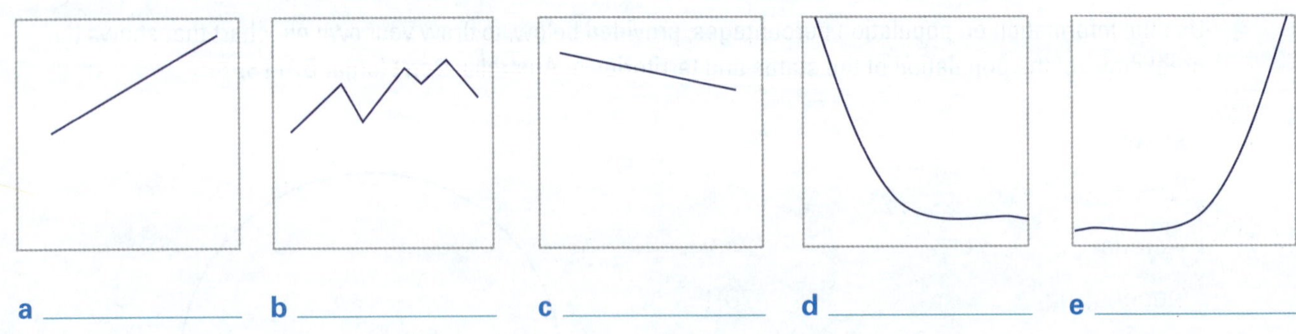

a ____________ b ____________ c ____________ d ____________ e ____________

ISBN 9780170367073

EXAMPLE OF A LINE GRAPH

2 Use the graph of Urbanisation rates below to answer the following questions.

a The graph's title is ______________________________.

b Dates are along the ______________ axis.

c All lines show ______________________________.

d Which country has the lowest percentage of urbanisation? ______________

e In what year did world urbanisation reach 50 per cent? ______________

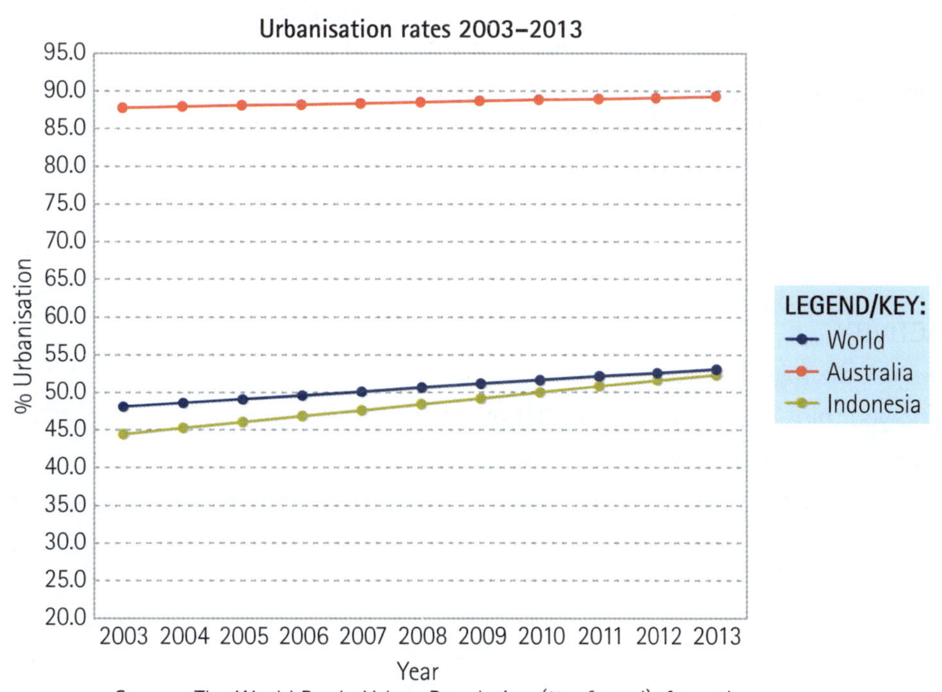

UNIT 9
SCATTER GRAPHS

A **scatter graph** shows relationships between two sets of data named on the *x* and *y* axes. They are drawn to see if different data have anything in common. The sets of data are called **variables**.

If the points appear to form a line (either straight or curved) in a particular direction, it is safe to say there is a relationship between them.

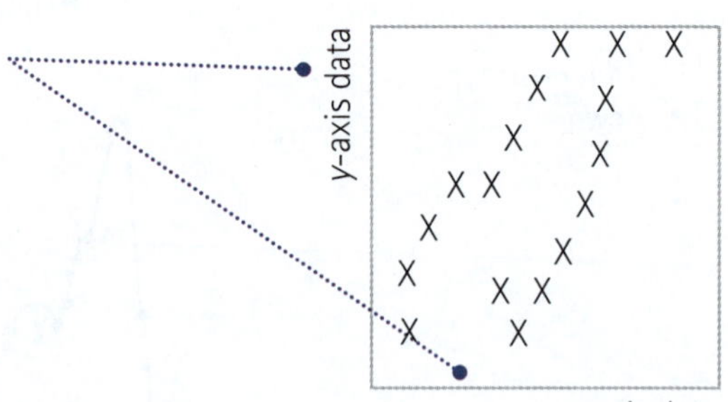

Line of best fit

To check for a straight line relationship:

- put a ruler along the scatter points until about half the points are on one side of the ruler and half the scatter points are on the other side of the ruler – there may be points that are on the line
- draw a line along the ruler.

  The line is called the **line of best fit** or the *trend line*.

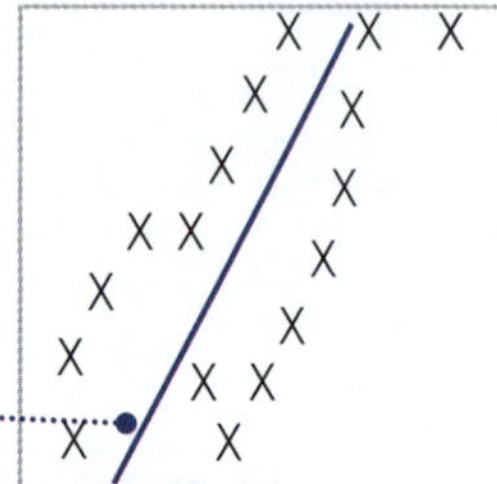

Different relationships

The trend line can be described in the same way as line graphs:

- if the line slopes up to the right, it is called a *positive relationship* – as one variable increases, so does the other variable; e.g. as the population of your town increases, there will be an increase in the number of new houses

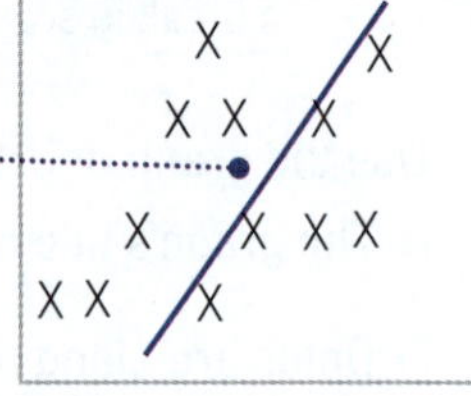

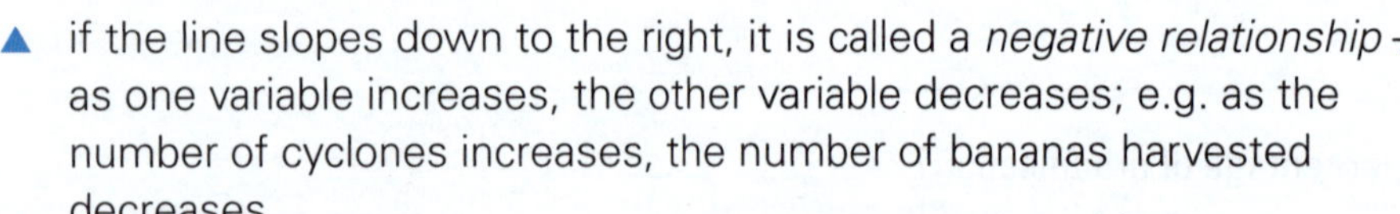

- if the line slopes down to the right, it is called a *negative relationship* – as one variable increases, the other variable decreases; e.g. as the number of cyclones increases, the number of bananas harvested decreases

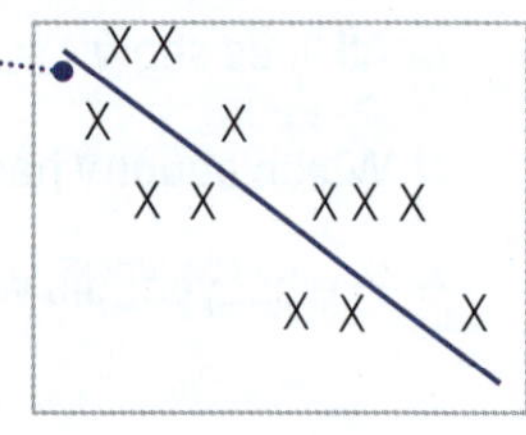

- if the points on the graph are too scattered to show a line, there is no relationship; e.g. the size of the coal deposit in Australia stays exactly the same, no matter how many industries want to use coal.

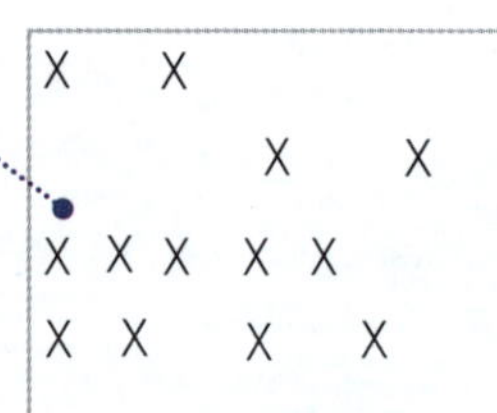

Exceptions (outliers) can be seen when one data point is a long way away from the rest of the data. This shows a place that does not fit the general pattern.

GROUP ACTIVITY

In pairs, discuss the following questions:

1 What do you think you know about scatter graphs now?
2 What questions or puzzles do you still have?
3 Where could you go for help to find a solution to your question or puzzle about scatter graphs?

 ISBN 9780170367073

1 Write positive, negative or none below each scatter graph to describe what type of relationship is shown.

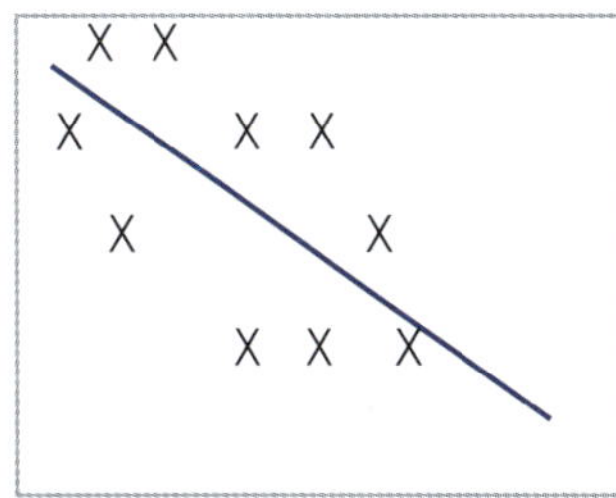

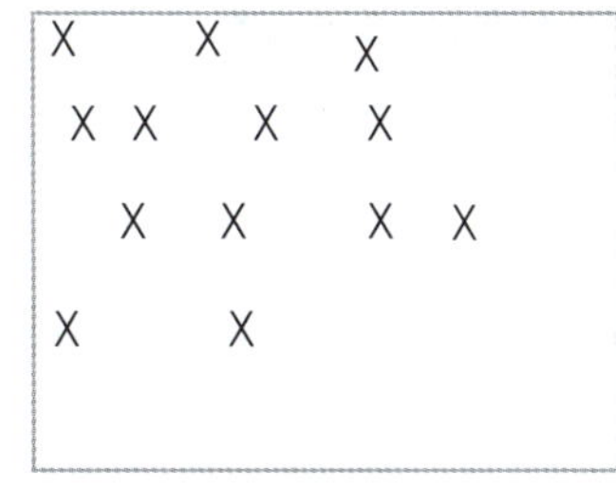

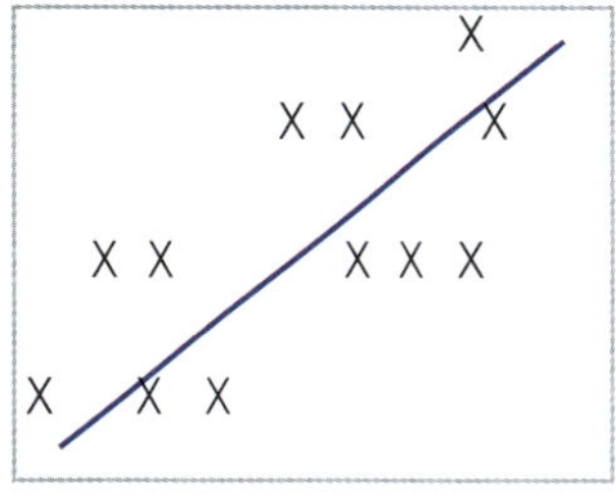

a ____________ **b** ____________ **c** ____________

2 Look at the graph below and fill in the gaps in the following sentences.

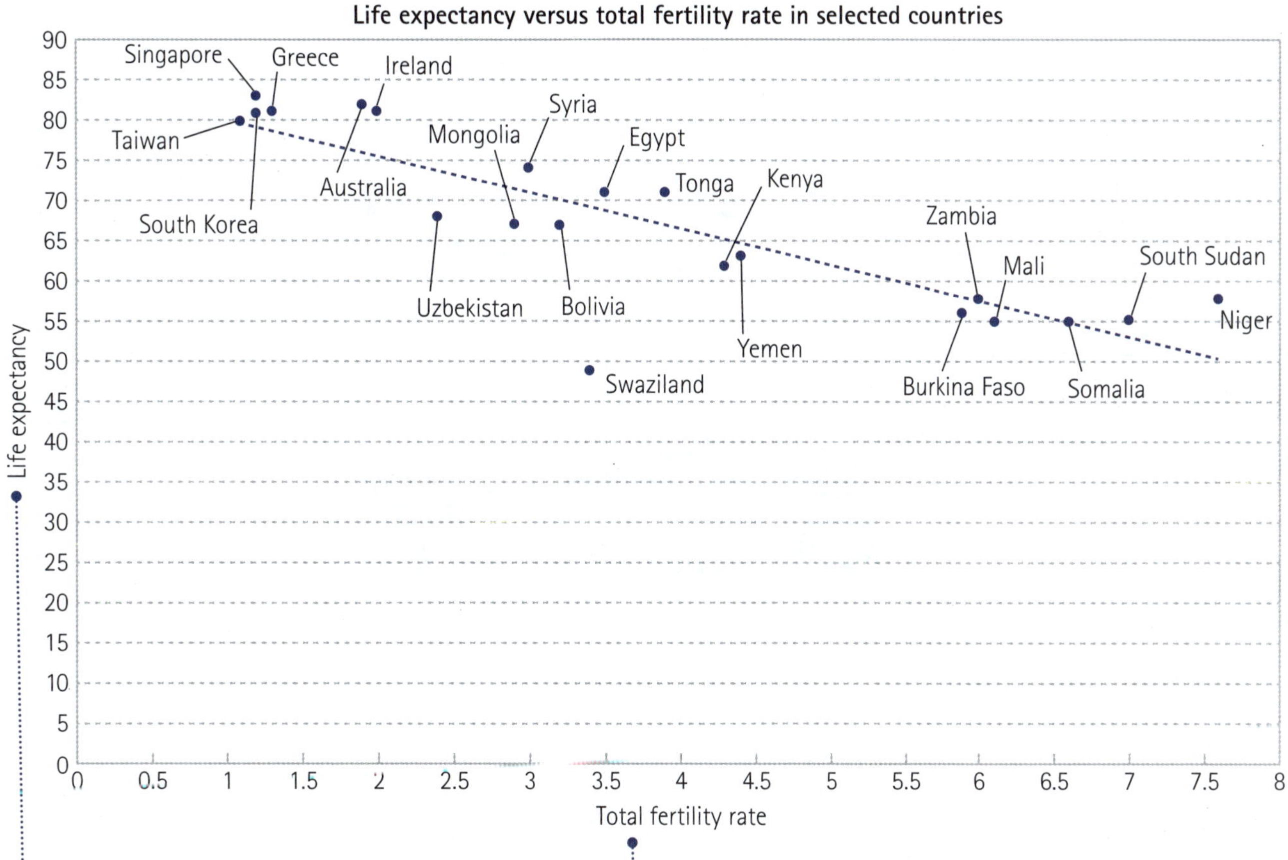

Life expectancy versus total fertility rate in selected countries

Singapore
Greece
Ireland
Taiwan
Syria
Mongolia
Egypt
Australia
Tonga
Kenya
South Korea
Zambia
Mali
South Sudan
Uzbekistan
Bolivia
Niger
Yemen
Swaziland
Burkina Faso
Somalia

Life expectancy: 0, 5, 10, 15, 20, 25, 30, 35, 40, 45, 50, 55, 60, 65, 70, 75, 80, 85, 90

Total fertility rate: 0, 0.5, 1, 1.5, 2, 2.5, 3, 3.5, 4, 4.5, 5, 5.5, 6, 6.5, 7, 7.5, 8

Life expectancy – the number of years that the average newborn baby may expect to live

Total fertility rate – the average number of children that would be born to a woman over her lifetime

a The title of the graph is ____.

b The vertical axis shows ____________________________.

c The horizontal axis shows ____________________________.

d There are ____________ countries on the trend line.

e The type of relationship shown is ____________________.

f As life expectancy decreases, fertility rates ____________________.

g ____________________ is an exception to the pattern.

ISBN 9780170367073

UNIT 10

CLIMATE GRAPHS

A graph showing the general pattern of climate for an area is called a climograph.

Melbourne is a city in the south-east of Australia and in the Southern Hemisphere. This means it has a temperate climate. For example, its summer is warm to hot, its spring and autumn are mild and moist and its winter is cool and wet. This is what the climograph for Melbourne looks like.

EXAMPLE OF A CLIMOGRAPH

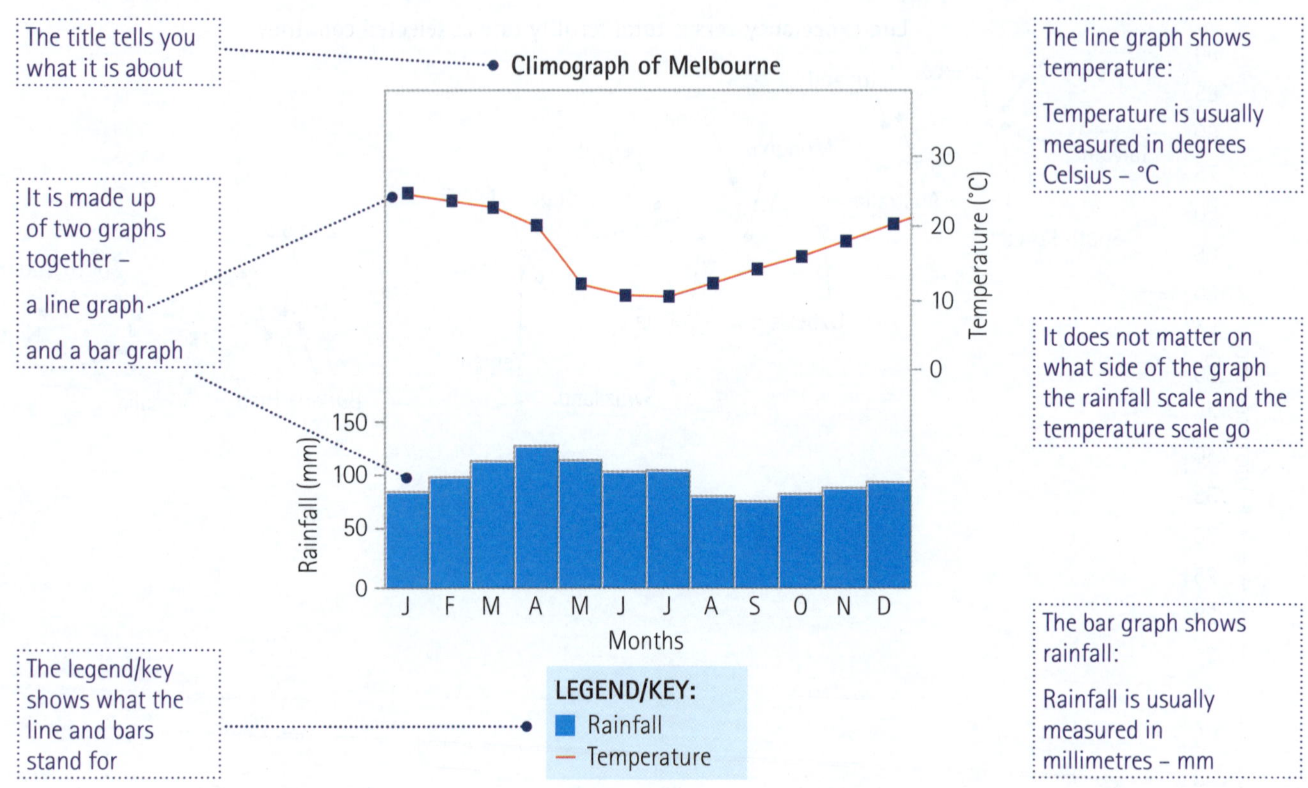

The temperatures and rainfall are the average figures for each month – called *mean temperature* and *rainfall*.

1 Use the climograph of Melbourne to fill in the gaps in the following sentences.

a The line graph shows ______________________________.

b The bar graph shows ______________________________.

c The measurement used to show rainfall is ______________________________.

d The measurement used to show temperature is ______________________________.

e The highest temperature is ____________ °C in the month of ______________________________.

f The lowest temperature is ____________ °C in the month of ______________________________.

g The highest rainfall is ____________ mm in the month of ______________________________.

h The lowest rainfall is ____________ mm in the month of ______________________________.

 ISBN 9780170367073

2 Use the climate data for Beijing (the capital of China) to fill out the climograph for Beijing. Colour it in. Don't forget BALTS.

MONTH	J	F	M	A	M	J	J	A	S	O	N	D
Temp. (°C)	−5	−2	5	14	20	25	26	25	20	13	4	3
Rainfall (mm)	4	5	8	17	35	78	243	141	58	16	11	3

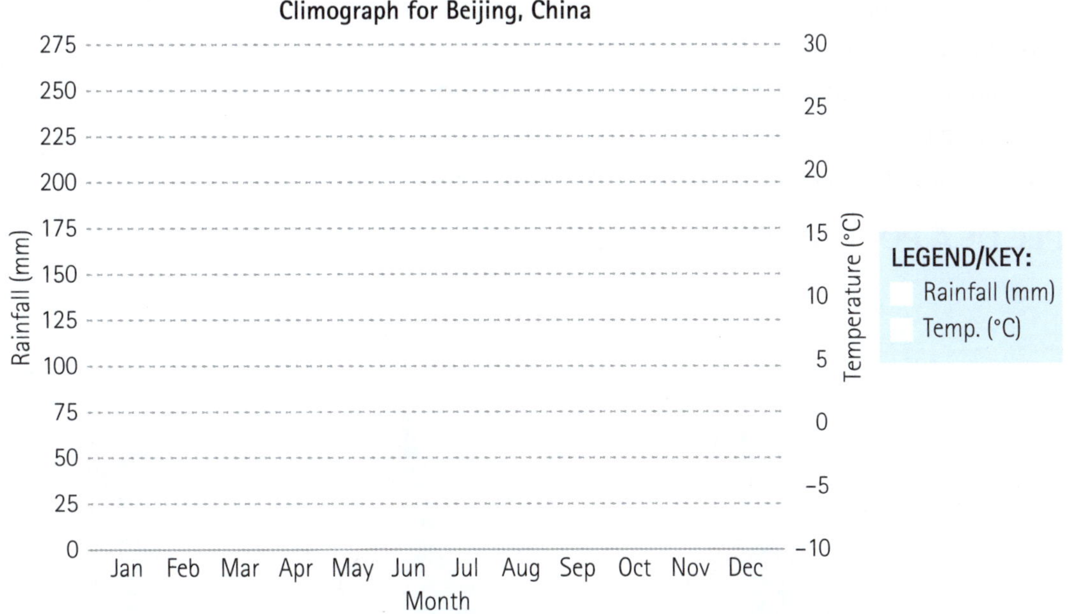

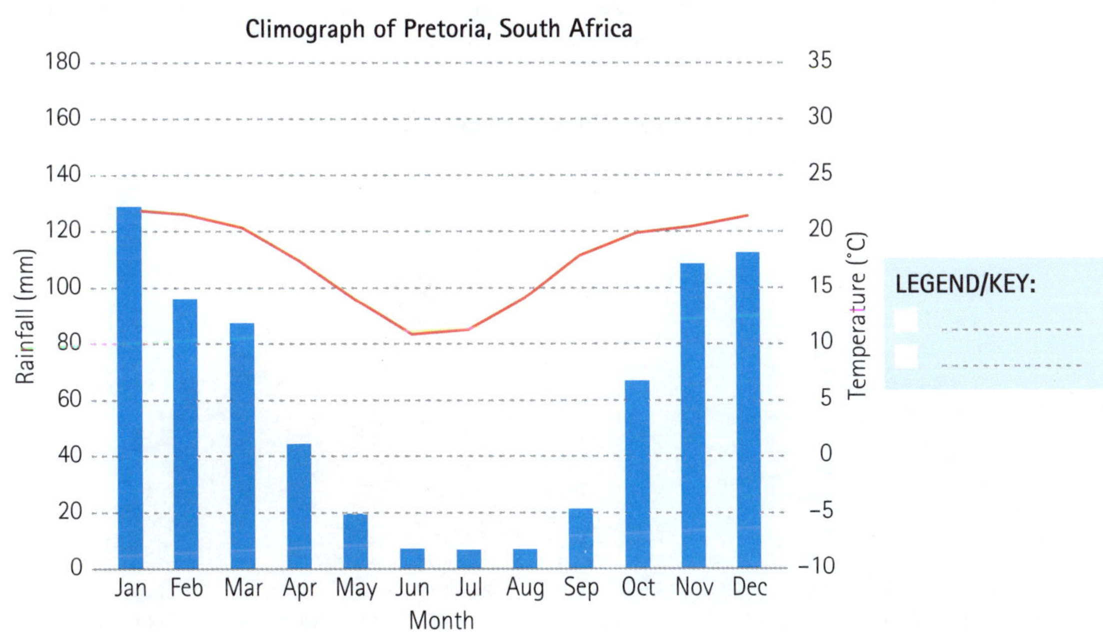

3 **a** Create a legend for the climograph of Pretoria (one of the capital cities of South Africa).

b The usual measurement for rainfall is ______________________.

c The usual measurement for temperature is ______________________.

d When is winter in Pretoria? ______________________

4 Circle the correct answer. Mean temperature means below average / average / above average.

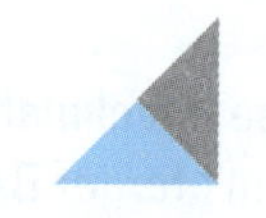

UNIT 11
POPULATION PYRAMIDS

Population pyramids will have different shapes depending on the type of population. For example:

- youthful/young population
- lots of children being born, but people dying quite young
- mature/ageing population
- not many children being born and people living a long life.

Population pyramid = a pyramid-shaped graph illustrating the age distribution of a population: the youngest are represented by a rectangle at the base; the oldest by one at the top.

EXAMPLE OF A POPULATION PYRAMID

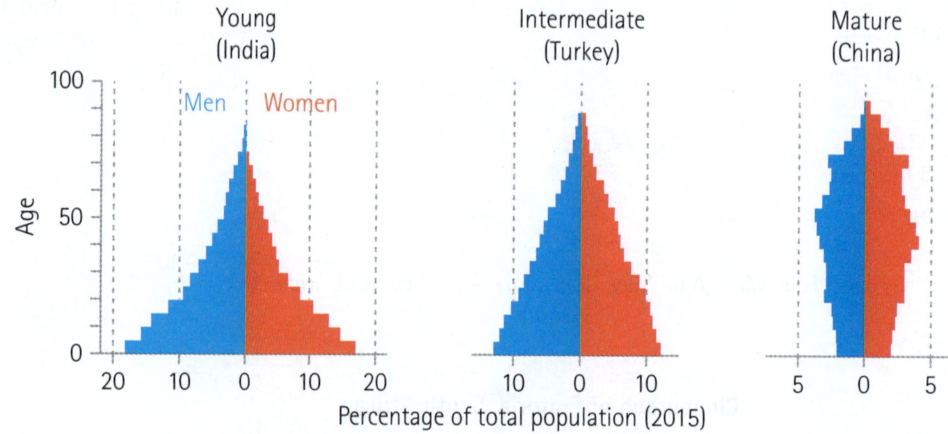

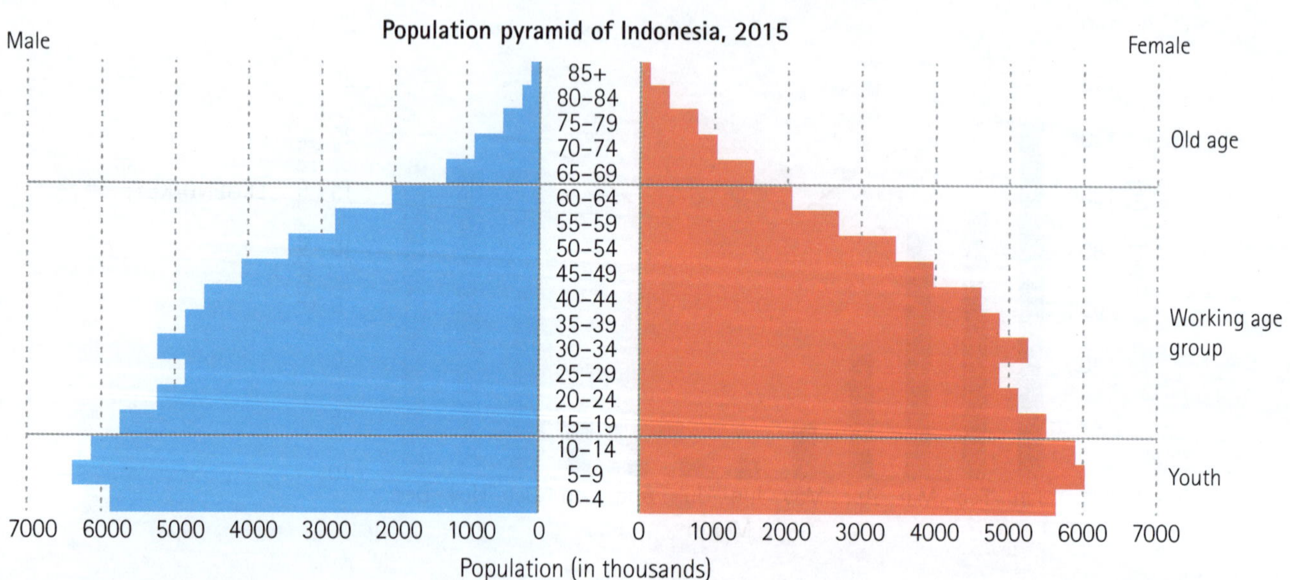

1 Look at the population pyramid of Indonesia for 2015 and fill in the gaps in the following sentences.

a The ages are marked on the ________________ axis and the population on the ________________ axis.

b Each bar is divided into ________________ on the left and ________________ on the right.

c The working age group goes from __________ to __________ and the youth section goes from __________ to __________, while the old age section goes from __________ to __________.

 ISBN 9780170367073

2 Study the population pyramid of Indonesia for 2015 and answer the following questions. Round figures off to the nearest 100 000.

a The total number of children aged 0–4 is ________________.

b The number of males aged 35–39 is ________________.

c The number of females aged 65–69 is ________________.

d Which age group has the largest number of people? ________________

3 Use the information in the table and the axis provided to draw a population pyramid for the Indigenous Australian population. Use a ruler. Colour the female side red (or pink) and the male side blue.

Population structure for Aboriginal and Torres Strait Islander people

	Males %	Females %
4 years and under	12.7	11.9
5–9 years	12.3	11.4
10–14 years	12.2	11.4
15–19 years	11.3	10.3
20–24 years	8.6	8.4
25–29 years	7.0	7.2
30–34 years	5.9	6.2
35–39 years	6.0	6.4
40–44 years	5.8	6.5
45–49 years	5.0	5.5
50–54 years	4.3	4.6
55–59 years	3.3	3.5
60–64 years	2.4	2.6
65–69 years	1.5	1.7
70–74 years	0.9	1.1
75 years and over	1.0	1.4

Source: Based on Australian Bureau of Statistics data

Male		Female
	75+	
	70–74	
	65–69	
	60–64	
	55–59	
	50–54	
	45–49	
	40–44	
	35–39	
	30–34	
	25–29	
	20–24	
	15–19	
	10–14	
	5–9	
	0–4	

14 12 10 8 6 4 2 0 0 2 4 6 8 10 12 14

Percentage of the population

4 Using the population pyramid you have drawn above, consider the services that would be needed to help support this population to grow into the future. Write down the three services you think would be most beneficial. Different factors to consider would be Economic, Education and Health.

____

____

____

UNIT 12
DEMOGRAPHIC TRANSITION MODEL

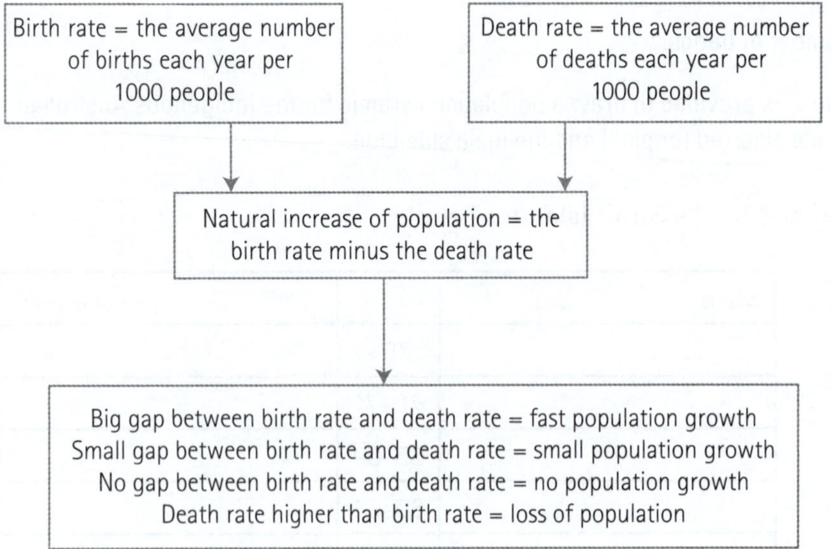

Demographic transition model = how a country's population changes over time. Demographics is the study of and writing about statistics of population (from the Greek words *demos* meaning 'people' and *graphy* meaning 'to write'). Demographic transition models show:

- the change in the structure of the population of a country over time
- the change in the level of development of the country over time.

There are five stages in the demographic transition model. A country will belong to one of these stages at a particular time. As the population of the country changes, and the country develops economically, the country will move into another stage of the model. The first stage of the model is mostly theoretical and only exists in isolated indigenous tribes.

1 **a** Colour in the natural increase on the demographic transition model on the opposite page.

b Colour in the table below the demographic transition model graph on the opposite page.

red = birth rate, blue = death rate, yellow = natural increase rate, green = technology

2 Use the information provided in the demographic transition model to fill in the gaps in the following sentences.

a Australia has a low birth rate, low death rate, low natural increase rate and established technology. This means it is at stage ________________ on the model.

b In 1900, most countries in South-East Asia were at stage 1. This meant they had ________________ birth rates, ________________ death rates, ________________ natural increase rates and ________________ technology.

c By 2010, Japan was at stage 5. This meant it had a ________________ birth rate, a ________________ death rate, a ________________ natural increase rate, and ________________ technology.

3 Write down the stage to which the following social situations are most likely to belong.

a A population explosion caused by a sudden improvement in health. ________________

b High urbanisation, not a lot of births, lots of new technology and education and mostly small families. ________________.

c A rural society of poor farmers and large families. ________________

ISBN 9780170367073

Demographic transition model

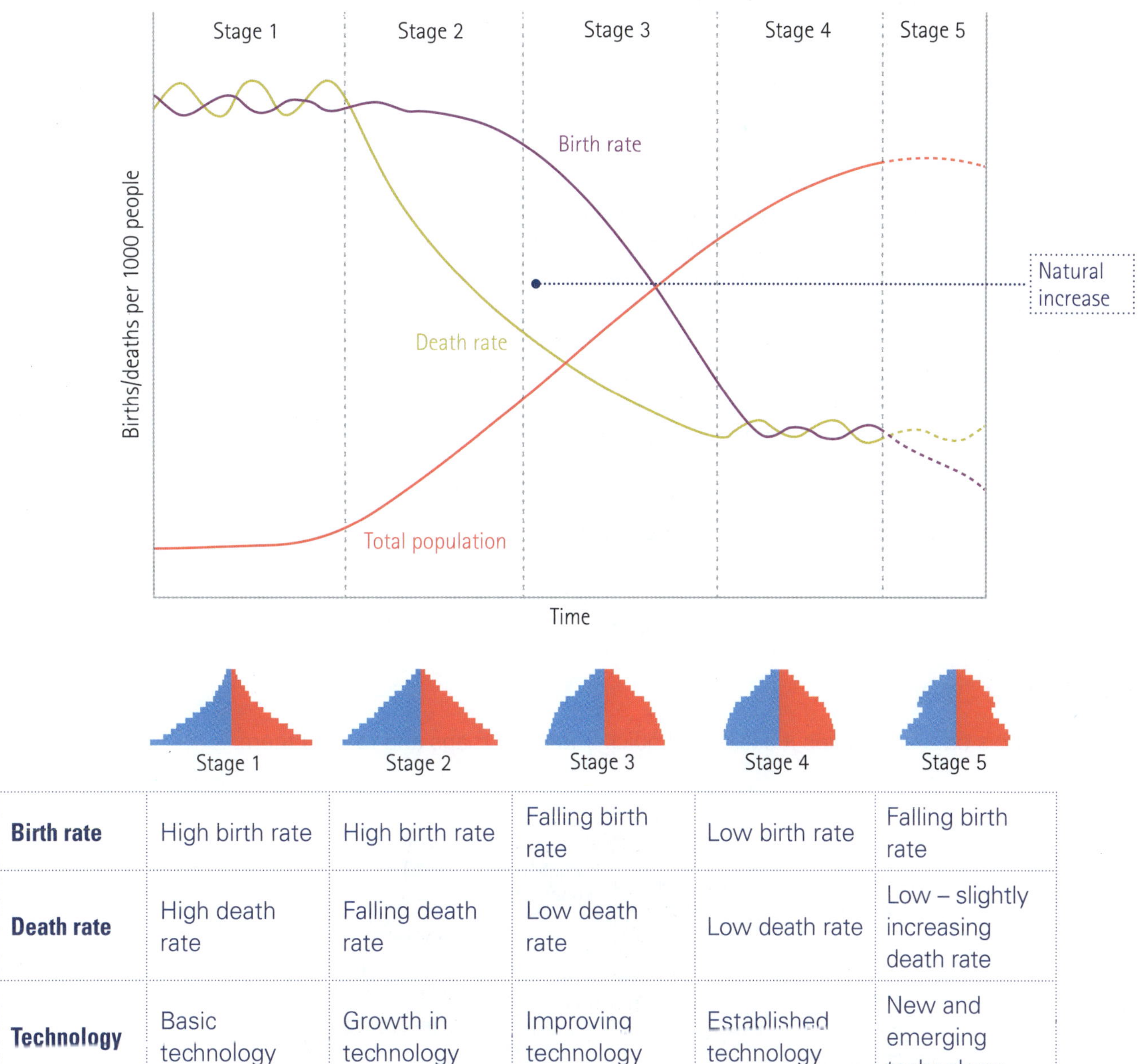

Birth rate	High birth rate	High birth rate	Falling birth rate	Low birth rate	Falling birth rate
Death rate	High death rate	Falling death rate	Low death rate	Low death rate	Low – slightly increasing death rate
Technology	Basic technology	Growth in technology	Improving technology	Established technology	New and emerging technology
Natural increase	Low natural increase	Rising natural increase	Rapid natural increase	Low natural increase	Low – negative natural increase
Example	Isolated indigenous communities	The Gambia	Brazil	USA	Japan

GROUP ACTIVITY

In groups of three or four, investigate the population in The Gambia or Brazil.

1. Without looking at any sources of information, what assumptions would you make about life for people (e.g. Are they rich or poor? Are the happy or sad? Are they healthy or unhealthy? Do they have enough food?) in that country based on the information provided in the table above.
2. For each of the headings in the table above (Birth rate, Death rate, Technology and Natural increase) outline the facts specific to the country you are investigating.
3. Then research one person's story about their life and experiences in the country you have chosen.
4. Refer back to the assumptions that you made about life in that country. Which of your ideas have changed based on the new information you have collected?

ISBN 9780170367073

UNIT 13
WHAT IS A MAP?

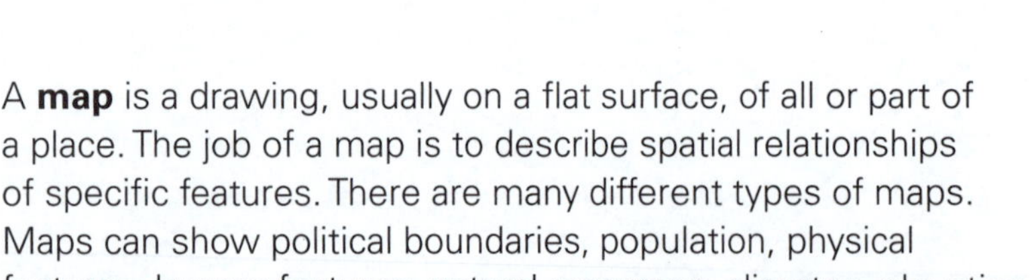

A **map** is a drawing, usually on a flat surface, of all or part of a place. The job of a map is to describe spatial relationships of specific features. There are many different types of maps. Maps can show political boundaries, population, physical features, human features, natural resources, climates, elevation (**topography**) and economic activities.

Maps are drawn to scale to make the drawing smaller than the actual place. For example, if you wanted to visit Brisbane and had a map that was the same size as the area, you wouldn't be able to fit it, and yourself, into your car. So the map has to be much smaller than the actual area.

To show all the things on the ground and where they are in relation to each other, the map needs to be from a bird's-eye view – what a bird sees from above.

A good map should have all of the elements listed in the box to the right (think BOLTSS to help you remember).

BOLTSS

B = Border: a line drawn around the map shows where the mapped area stops

O = Orientation: direction arrow showing where north is

L = Legend: key showing the symbols and features on the map

T = Title: name at top (sometimes bottom) of the map to show what the map is about

S = Scale: words or figures or lines to show how much smaller the map is than the actual place

S = Source: where the map comes from and when

EXAMPLES OF MAPS

Using symbols on maps makes it easier and quicker to draw maps and to read them.

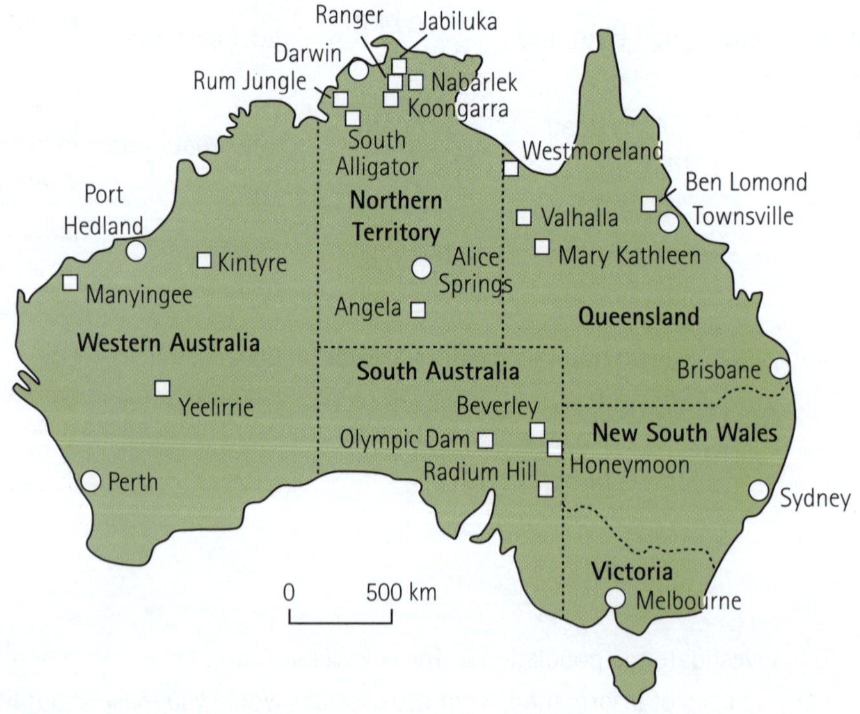

1 Colour the map above to show:
mine = red
city/town = yellow.

2 On the same map, add:
a A legend **b** A border **c** An orientation arrow **d** A title

ISBN 9780170367073

3 Look at the map of Queenscliff below and create a legend. Find the following features on the map and draw the corresponding symbol from the map in the box provided. Ensure your legend colours match the map given.

a Main road ☐	**b** Bike track ☐	**c** Bus route ☐
d Walking track ☐	**e** Telephone ☐	**f** Lookout ☐
g Information ☐	**h** Parking area ☐	**i** Church ☐

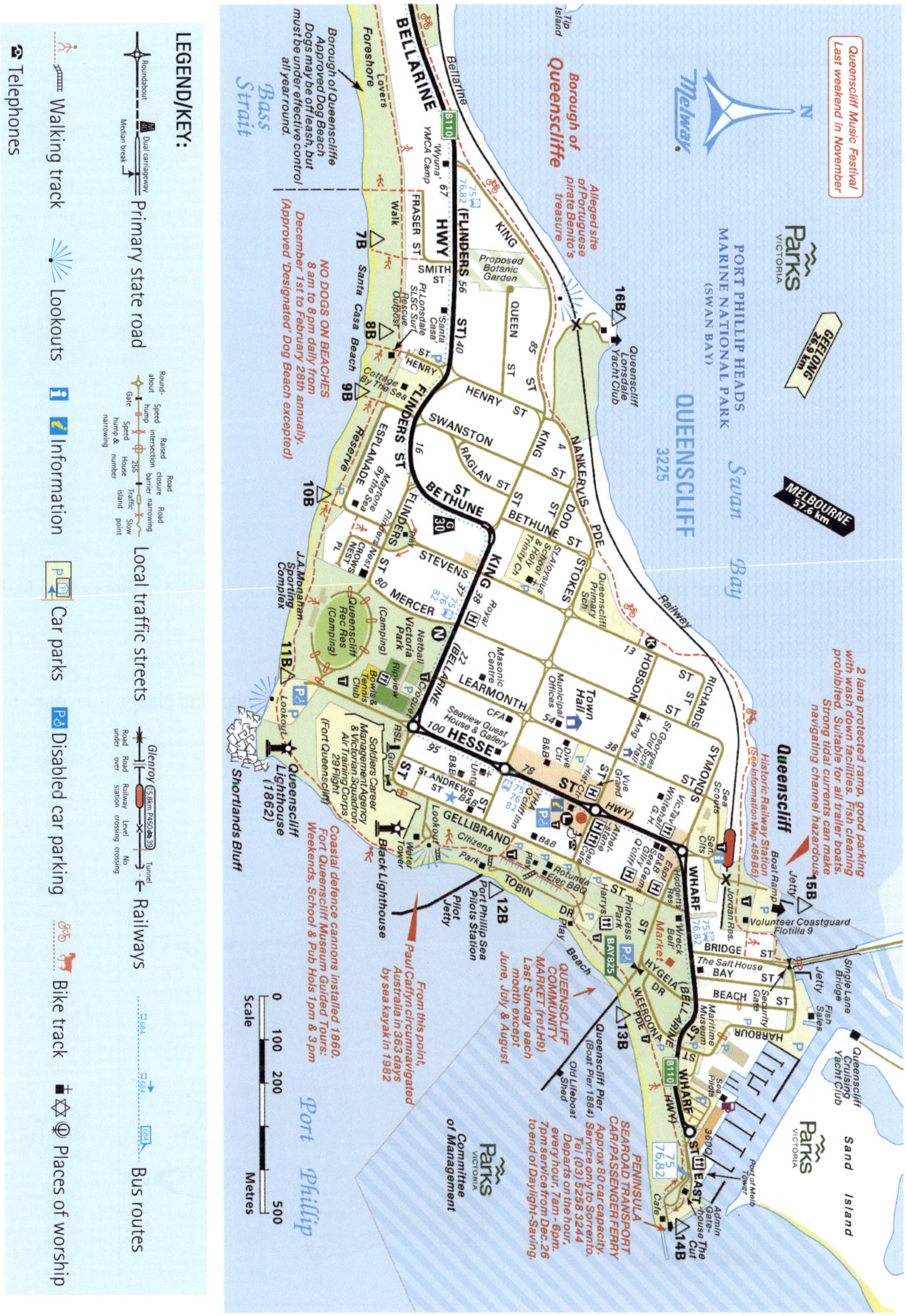

Map proudly reproduced with permission from Melway Street Directory

UNIT 14
DIRECTIONS

The main (cardinal) compass points are: **N** (north), **E** (east), **S** (south), **W** (west).

This compass rose has eight points.

It could be further divided into 16 points to make it even more accurate.

direction = the point towards which you face or move

compass = an instrument used to find direction; it has a magnetised needle that always points to magnetic north

compass rose = the symbol on a map that shows the direction of north; its name comes from the way points of a compass look like the arrangement of petals of a rose flower

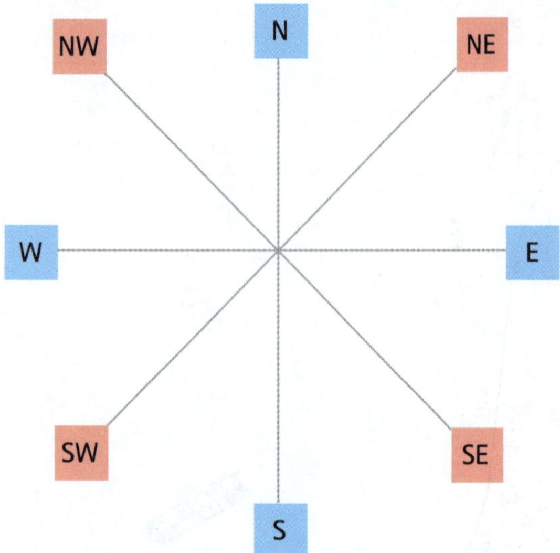

1 Add the following compass points to the diagram of the compass rose. They are in order of where they fit. For example, NNE fits between N and NE.
NNE, ENE, ESE, SSE, SSW, WSW, WNW, NNW

2 Use the map of Volcano Island below to work out the direction of each of the following places from each other.

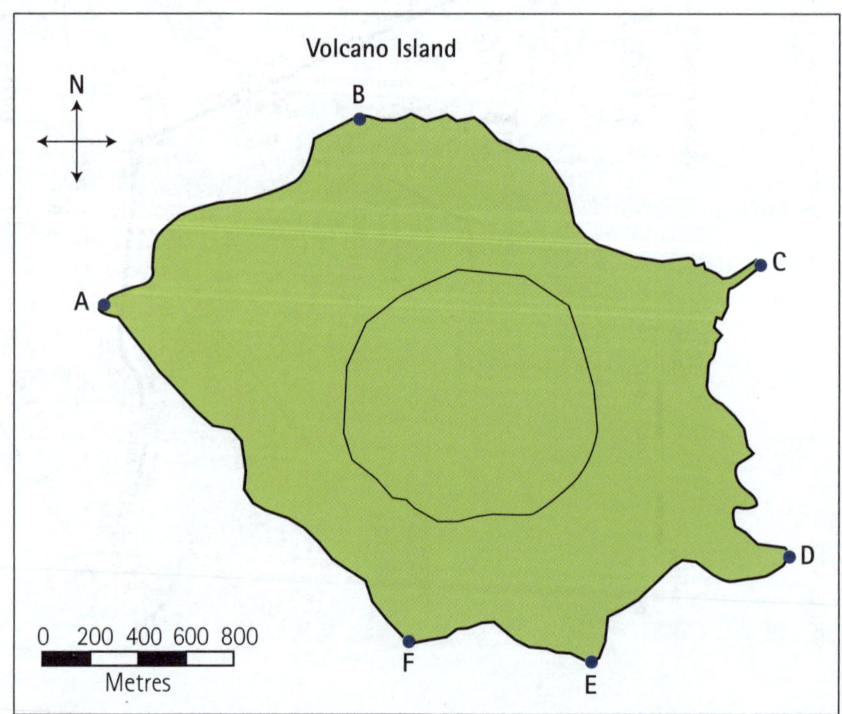

a A–B ____________ **b** D–C ____________ **c** A–F ____________

ISBN 9780170367073

3 Write the directions of these arrows on the answer lines below.

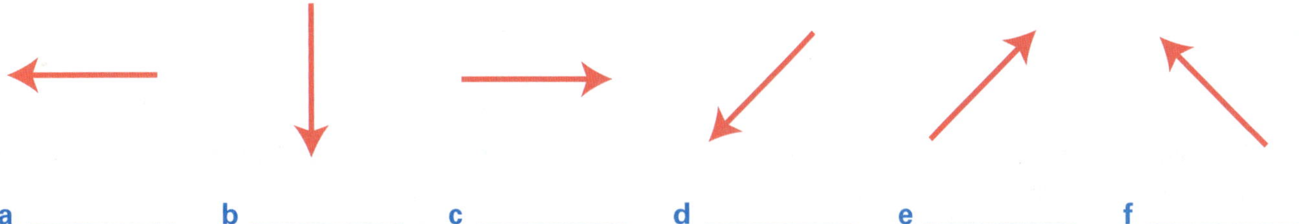

a ________ b ________ c ________ d ________ e ________ f ________

4 Yan is 12 years old. He believes in sustainability. He thinks his generation should use resources wisely so there will be resources left for future generations. The sketch map below shows a farm he would like to create one day.

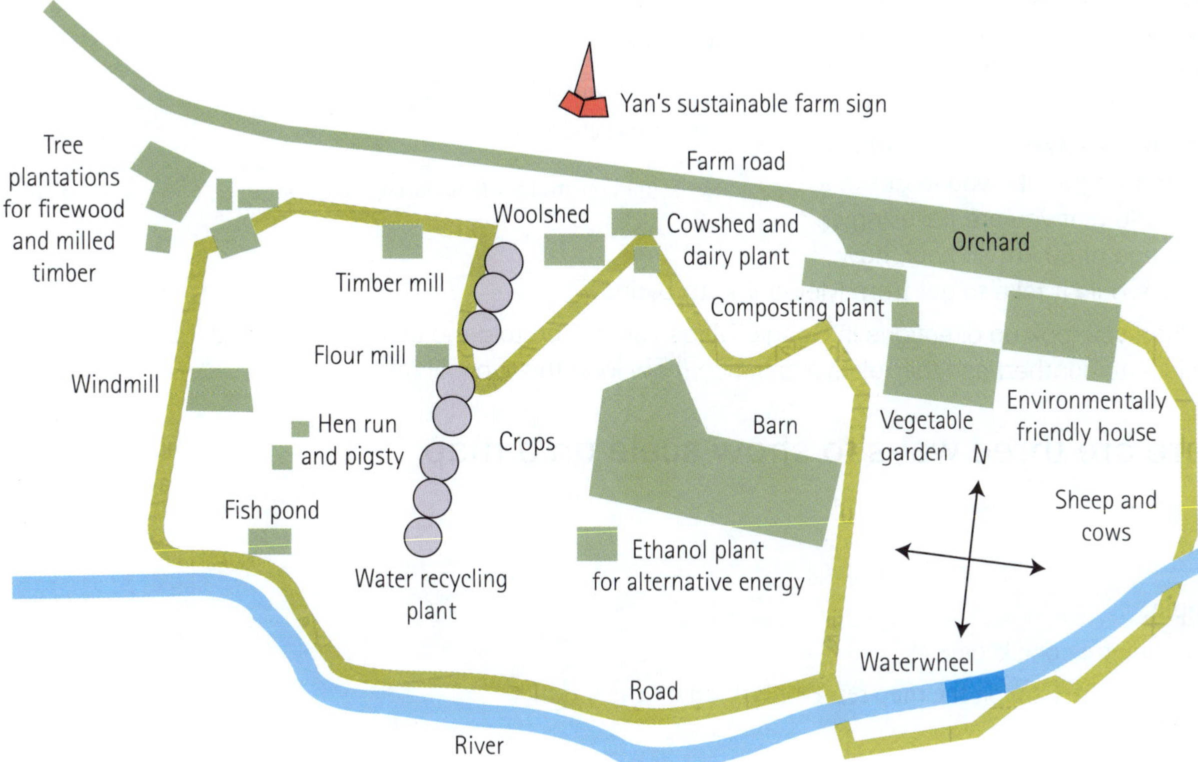

a Circle the letters of BOLTSS that are missing from the map:

B O L T S S

Circle the correct answer from the words in green below.

b The sustainable farm sign is north / south of the crops.

c The fish pond is east / west of the waterwheel.

d The cow shed and dairy plant are north-east / north-west of the flour mill.

e The water recycling plant is south-east / south-west of the composting plant.

ISBN 9780170367073

UNIT 15
SCALE AND DISTANCE

The **scale** on a map relates to the relationship (or ratio) between distance on a map and the corresponding distance on the ground in real life.

The way to show how much smaller a map is than the actual area of a place is to use a scale.

The scale on a map shows you:

- what distance one centimetre on the map represents on the ground in real life (e.g. every centimetre on the map represents 100 km on the ground)
- **absolute distance** – how close or far apart places are (e.g. how many kilometres from Sydney to Melbourne)
- **relative distance** to time – how long it might take you to get to a place (e.g. if you are travelling an average of 80 km an hour, how long would it take to get from Melbourne to Sydney?)

Via M31	8 h 30 min
8 h 20 min without traffic – show traffic	878 km
Via A41 and M31	10 h 51 min
Sydney, Australia – Melbourne, Australia	1 h 30 min

When you look up directions in Google Maps you will be told the absolute distance (how far it is from one place to another) and the relative distance (how long the trip will take).

There are three ways to show scale on a map

Words

Example:

one centimetre : one kilometre

This means that 1 cm on the map represents 1 km on the ground.

Ratio

Example:

1:100 000

This means that 1 cm on the map is the same as 100 000 cm on the ground.

To make this easier to understand we can say that 100 000 cm = 1 km, so the scale says 1 cm on the map represents 1 km on the ground.

Line

Example:

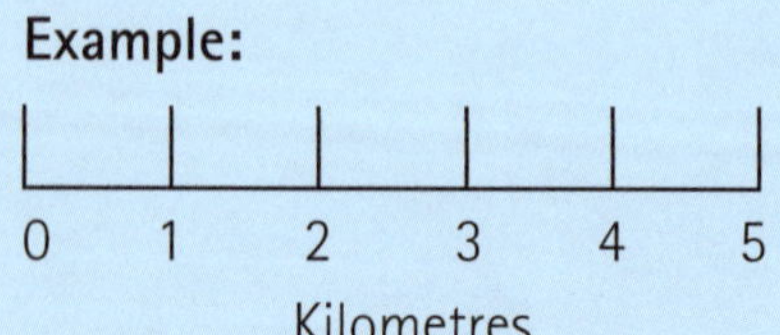

This means that 1 cm on the map is the same as 1 km on the ground.

ISBN 9780170367073

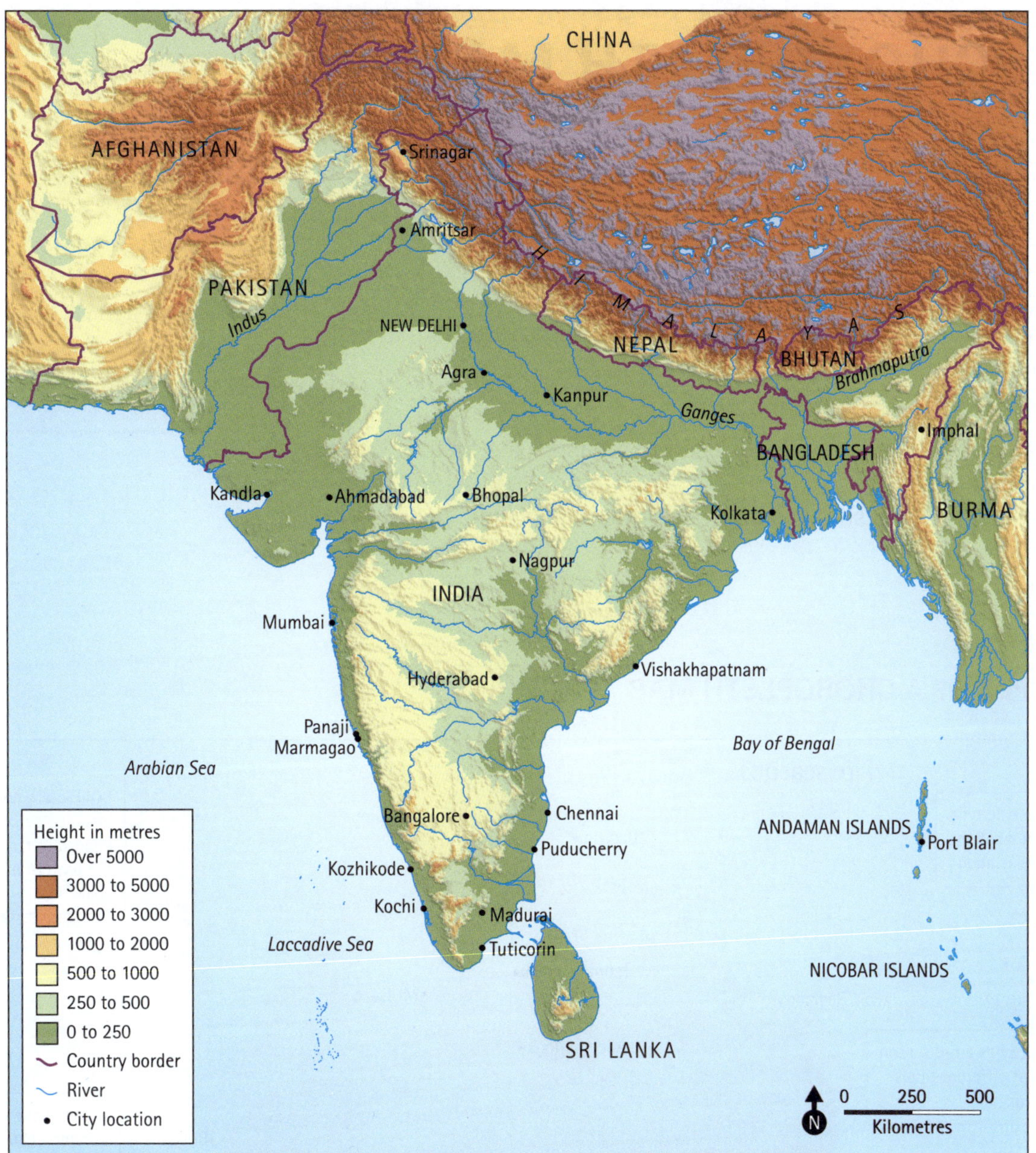

1 Look at the map of India.

a Which type of scale is shown on the map?

____

b Write down another two ways the scale could have been shown on the map.

____

____

2 Vertical height on this map is shown using colour to indicate scale. Which of these cities is the highest? Agra, Hyderabad or Nagpur?

3 Use Google Maps to find out the relative distance and absolute distance from your house to a friend's house.

a Relative distance ____________

b Absolute distance ____________

UNIT 16
CHOROPLETH MAPS

A choropleth map is a thematic map in which areas are shaded or patterned in proportion to the amount of the feature shown, e.g. population density or rainfall.

A choropleth map is used to show patterns across places that have:

- clear regions
- continuous values across the areas.

A percentage or a ratio value is used to measure the feature; not single numbers.

Common features shown on a choropleth map include:

- population
- rainfall
- fire ratings.

Choropleth comes from the Greek words *choros* meaning 'place' and *plethos* meaning 'multitude – a great number'. So choropleth means a graphic (a map) about a place showing information about groups of factors.

EXAMPLE OF A CHOROPLETH MAP

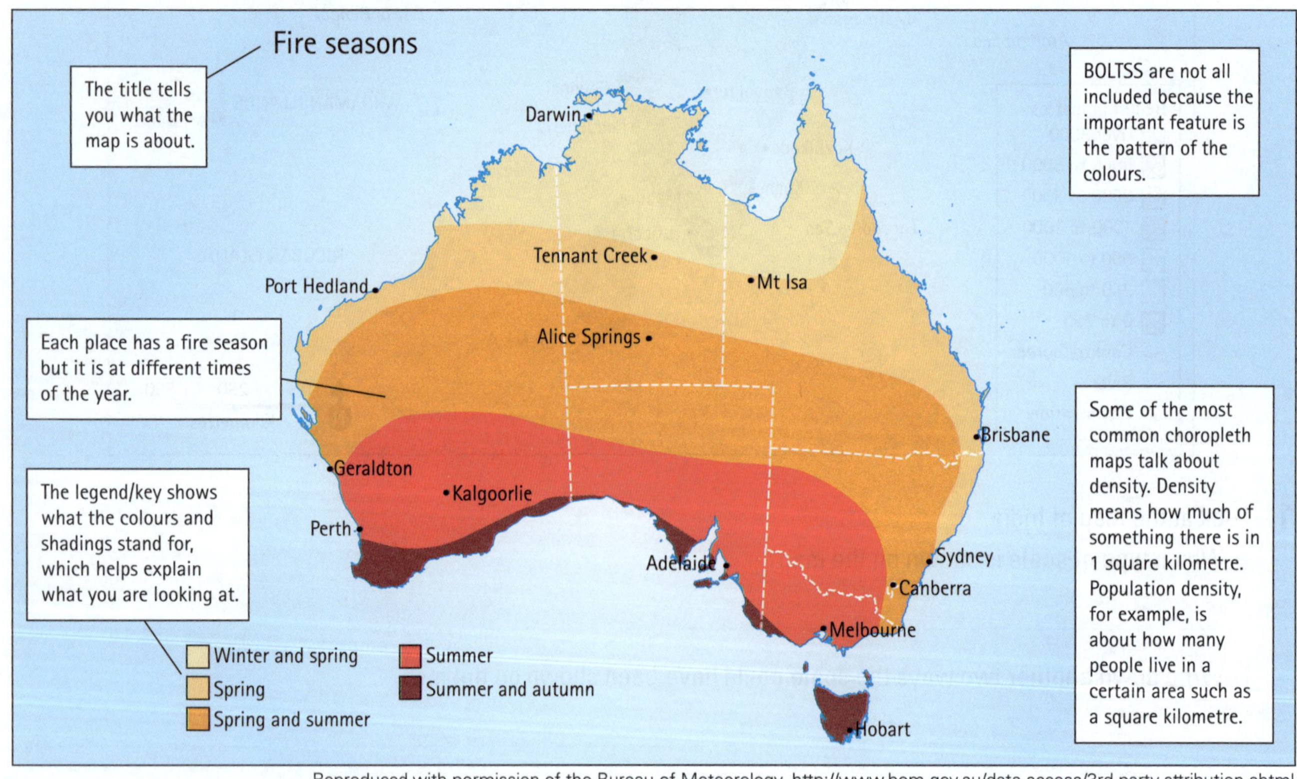

Reproduced with permission of the Bureau of Meteorology, http://www.bom.gov.au/data-access/3rd-party-attribution.shtml

When choosing the colours for a choropleth map, use one colour group, starting from light colours for the lower values to darker colours for the higher values. If you are using a pattern instead of a colour, start with a light pattern at the low end of the values and a solid block at the highest values. See opposite for some examples.

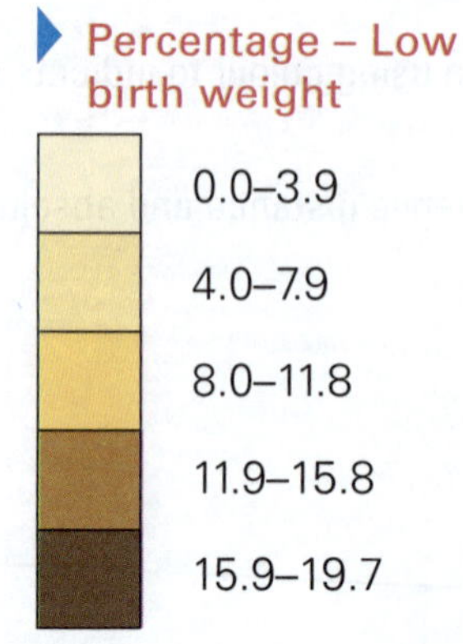

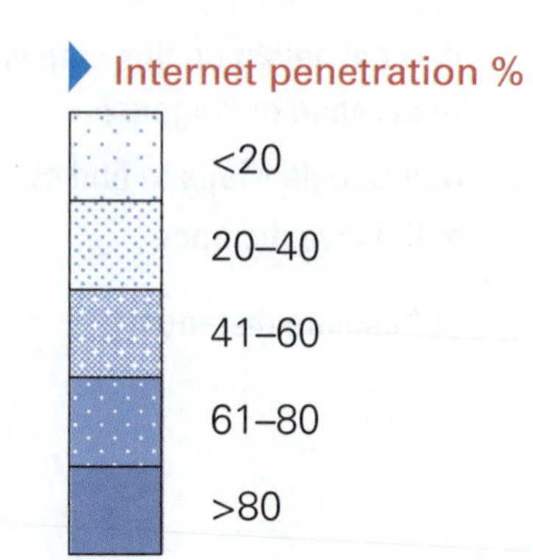

ISBN 9780170367073

1 Complete this choropleth map of Australia's population. Colour in the legend below for the map titled 'Percentage of Australia's population by state'. You can choose your own colours, but remember that the colours need to go from light to dark. Use the table below to help you know what colour each state should be.

State	%
New South Wales	32.0
Victoria	24.9
Queensland	20.1
South Australia	7.2
Western Australia	11.0
Tasmania	2.2
Northern Territory	1.0
Australian Capital Territory	1.6

Source: Based on Australian Bureau of Statistics data

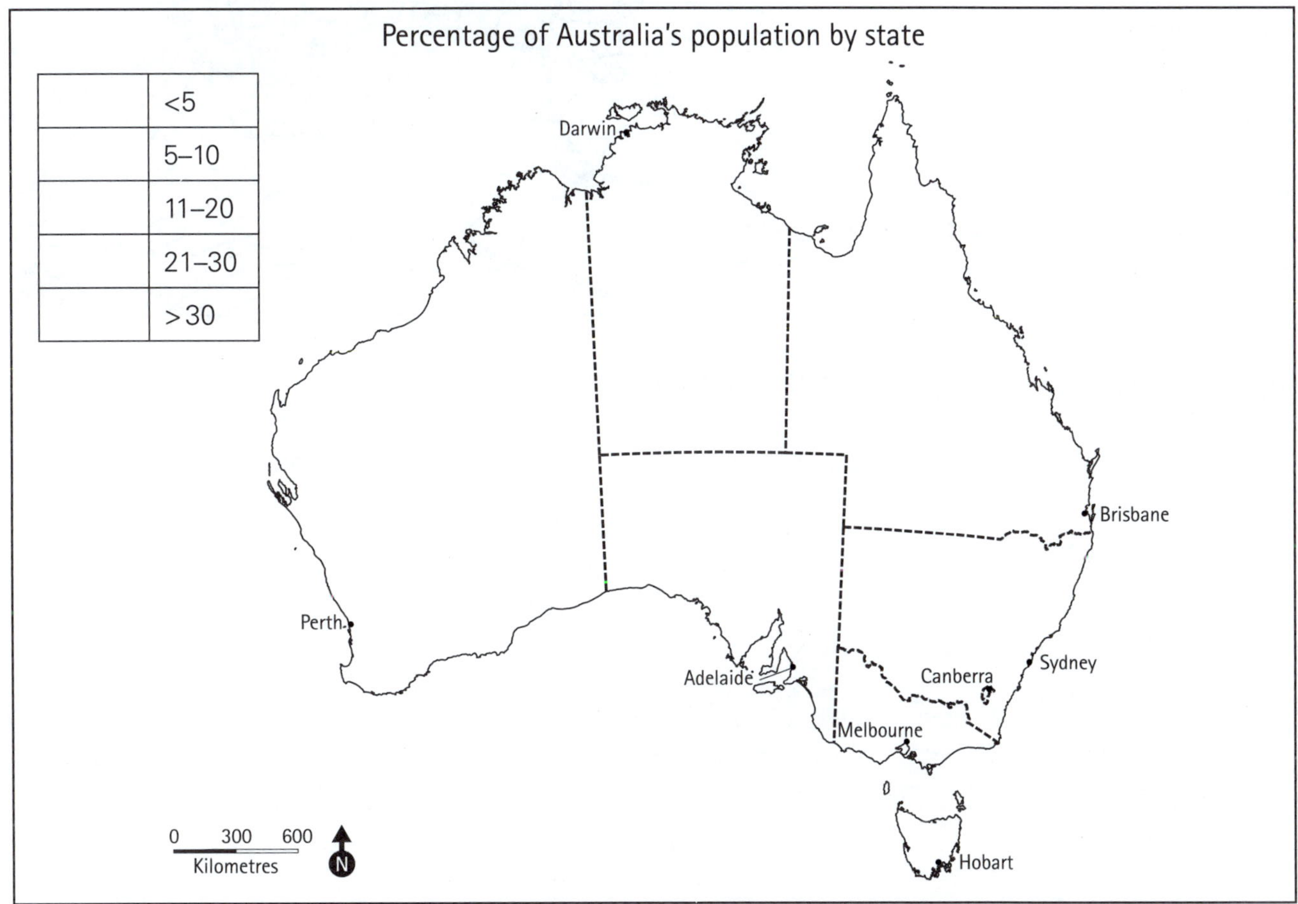

2 The following statements are about Australia's population. Tick the box if the statement is true or put a cross in the box if the statement is false.

a Population is spread unevenly over the country. ☐

b More people live in the west than in the east. ☐

c Victoria has the highest percentage of the population living in the east of Australia. ☐

d There is a greater percentage of the population living in Western Australia than South Australia. ☐

e A small number of people live in Tasmania. ☐

UNIT 17
WEATHER MAPS

Weather forecasters predict what the weather is going to be like. This is called the *weather forecast*. They do this by studying what is happening in the **atmosphere**. They use satellite images, radar images, weather balloons, computer simulations, statistics and instruments such as barometers, wind and rain gauges.

Atmosphere

Atmosphere:

- is the layers of gases that surround the world
- is called air by humans living on Earth
- can't be felt by humans, but does have weight
- puts pressure on earth
- its pressure is measured by a barometer
- its pressure is measured in millibars (mb) or hectopascals (hPa)
- its pressure is shown on weather maps as lines called isobars.

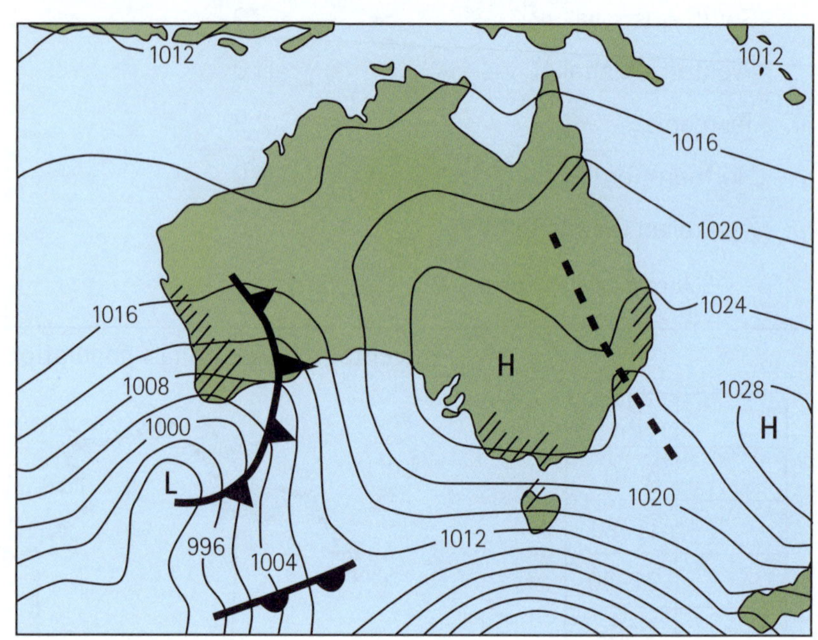

Special symbols on a weather map

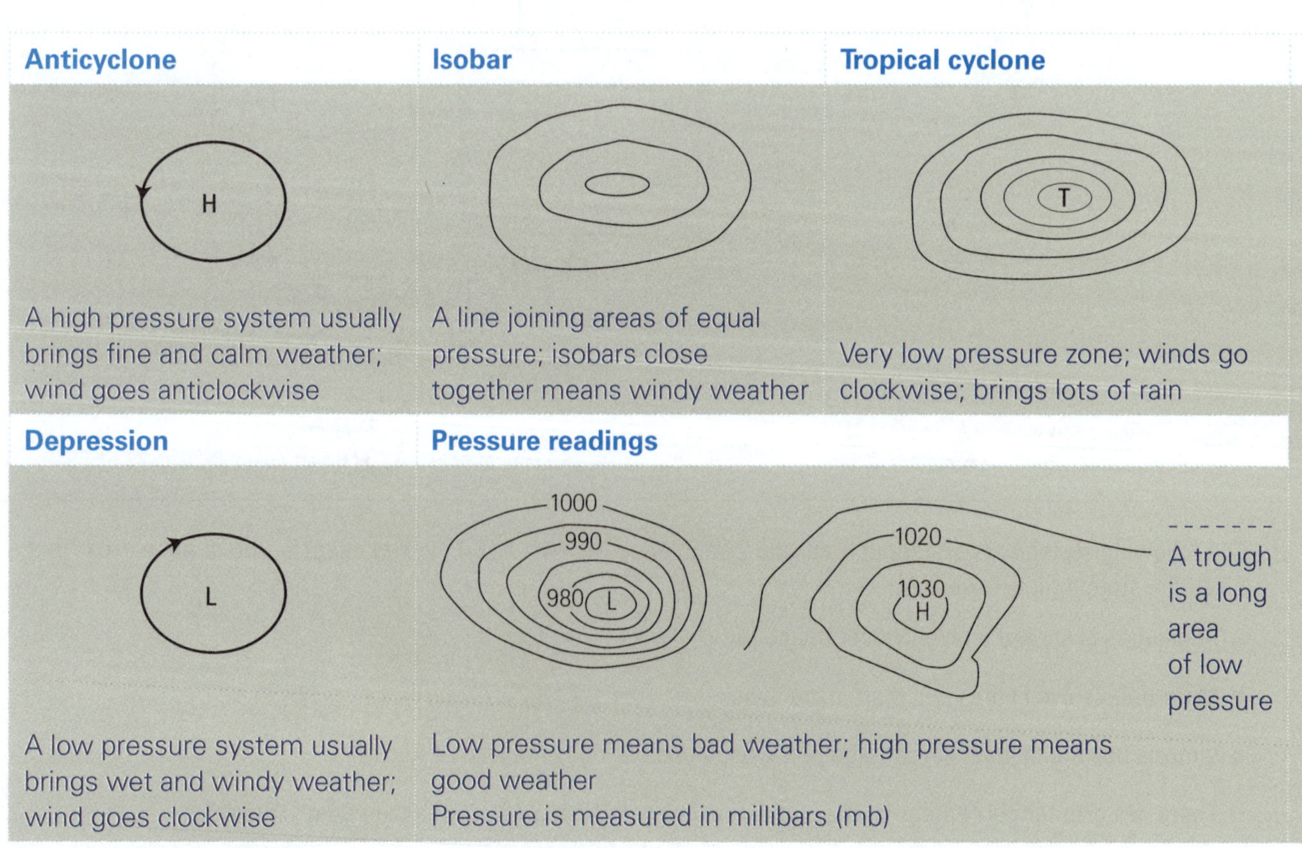

 ISBN 9780170367073

1 Look at the weather map opposite and write in the missing data.

a The H stands for ______________________.

b The L stands for ______________________.

c The name for the lines with numbers on them is ______________________.

d The map shows rain forecast (diagonal lines). Give the approximate location of this forecast rain.

____

____

e The interval between each line measurement is ______________________.

f The name for the measurements is ______________________.

g The two types of front shown are ______________________ and ______________________.

h The two types of front not shown are ______________________ and ______________________.

2 Cross out the wrong option in the following statements about the weather map.

a The weather in north Australia is expected to be fine / rainy tomorrow.

b There should be a slow breeze / fast wind tomorrow over most of Australia.

c The dotted line shows a trough / an anticyclone.

d The isobars at the south on the map are close together / far apart.

Front (marks the boundary between warm air and cold air)

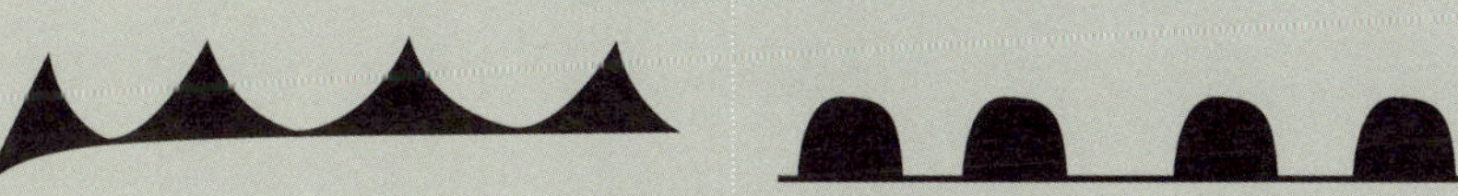

A **cold front** often brings rain

A **warm front** often brings drizzle

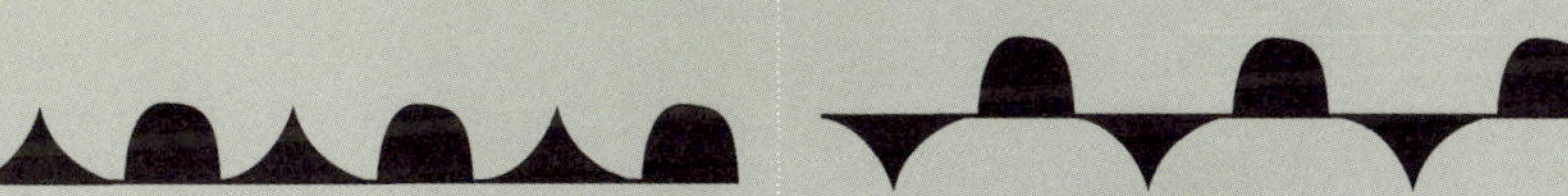

An **occluded front** occurs when a cold front catches up with a warm front, often bringing long rainy sessions

A **stationary front** involves no movement of air and brings long, continuous rainy sessions

Winds

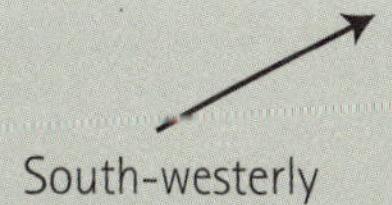

South-westerly

Northerly

Winds are named after the direction from which they are blowing; a wind blowing from the south-west is called a south-west wind or a south-westerly, while a wind blowing from the north is called a north wind or a northerly

Fast wind

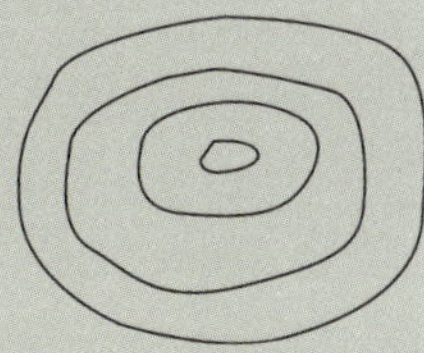

Slow wind

Fast winds are shown by isobars close together; slow winds are shown by isobars far apart

ISBN 9780170367073

UNIT 18
LATITUDE AND LONGITUDE

Latitude and longitude are the imaginary lines that run horizontally and vertically around the globe. They exist only on globes and maps. If you go to Greenwich in London you will be able to see the 0 degree line of longitude and stand with one foot on either side of it.

Lines of **latitude** are horizontal full circles of different sizes that run parallel to each other around the earth.

The **Equator** is the 0 degree line of latitude.

The equator divides the world into two **hemispheres** – the *Northern Hemisphere* and the *Southern Hemisphere*.

The other lines of latitude are north or south of the equator.

There are five main lines of latitude (see below).

The North Pole is 90 degrees north and the South Pole is 90 degrees south.

Lines of **longitude** run vertically and all cross at the North and South Poles. They are all the same length.

On the right you can see the Earth flattened to show the divisions between longitude lines. The 0 degree longitude line is called the **prime meridian** or **Greenwich meridian**. The Greenwich meridian and the 180-degree longitude line divide the world into two hemispheres called the *Eastern Hemisphere* and the *Western Hemisphere*.

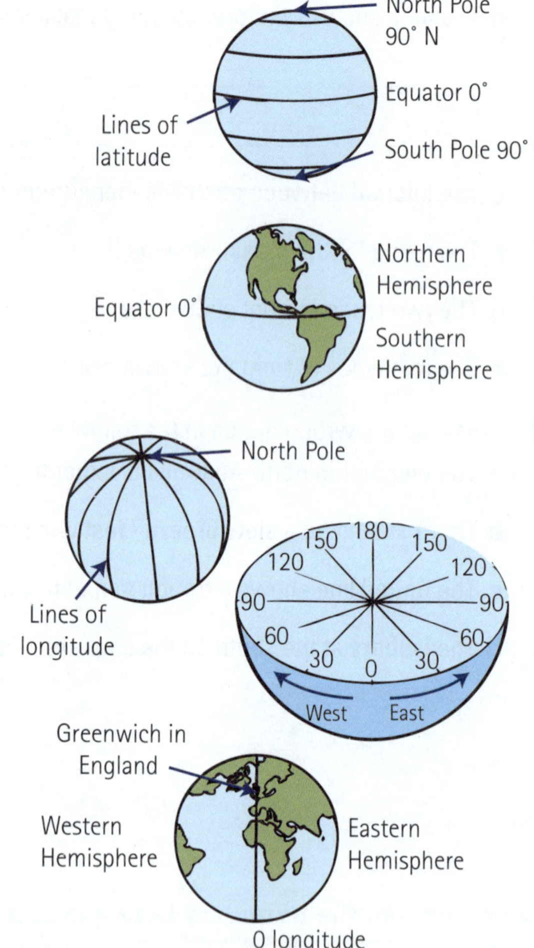

Five main lines of latitude

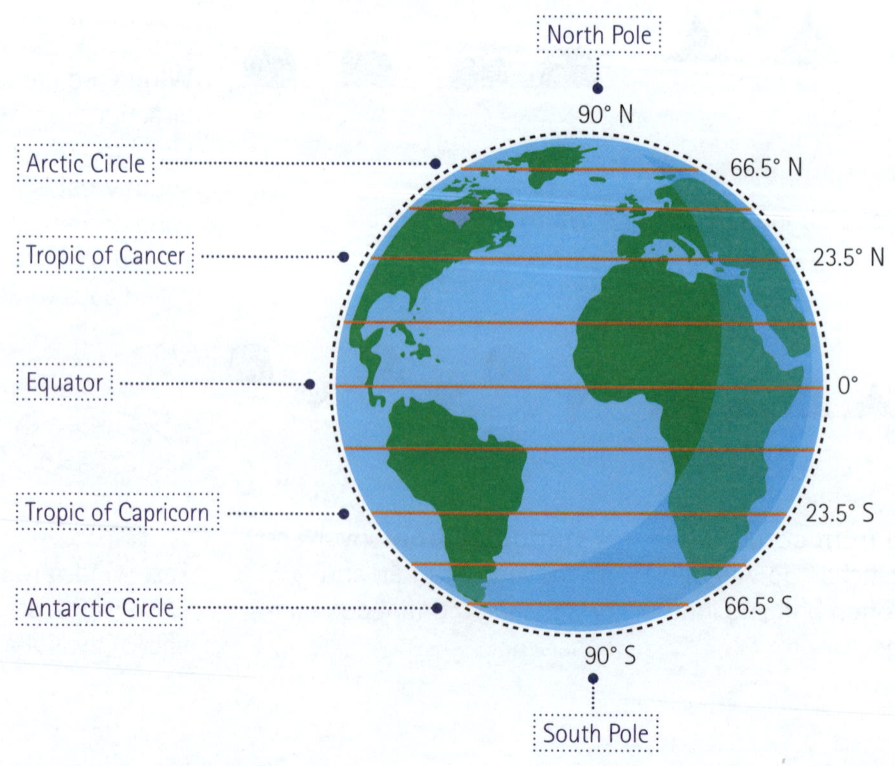

ISBN 9780170367073

1 Open Google Maps and put it in 'satellite' view. Enter the following latitude and longitude locations and see what you can locate. You may need to zoom in or out on your view to find the mystery object.

a 8 06 54 S 112 55 30 E Natural feature ________________ Country ________________

b 52 29 7 N 13 29 27 E Human feature ________________ Country ________________

c 51 22 21 N 1 50 51 W Animal ________________ Country ________________

2 Use the map of Australia in the Pacific below to fill in the following sentences.

a The numbers down the left side refer to lines of ________________.

b The numbers across the bottom refer to lines of ________________.

c The latitude line 'through' New Zealand is ________________ degrees.

d The place closest to the intersection between the 30 degrees south line and the 160 degrees east line is ________________.

e The dotted line running through Australia is the ________________________.

Australia in the Pacific

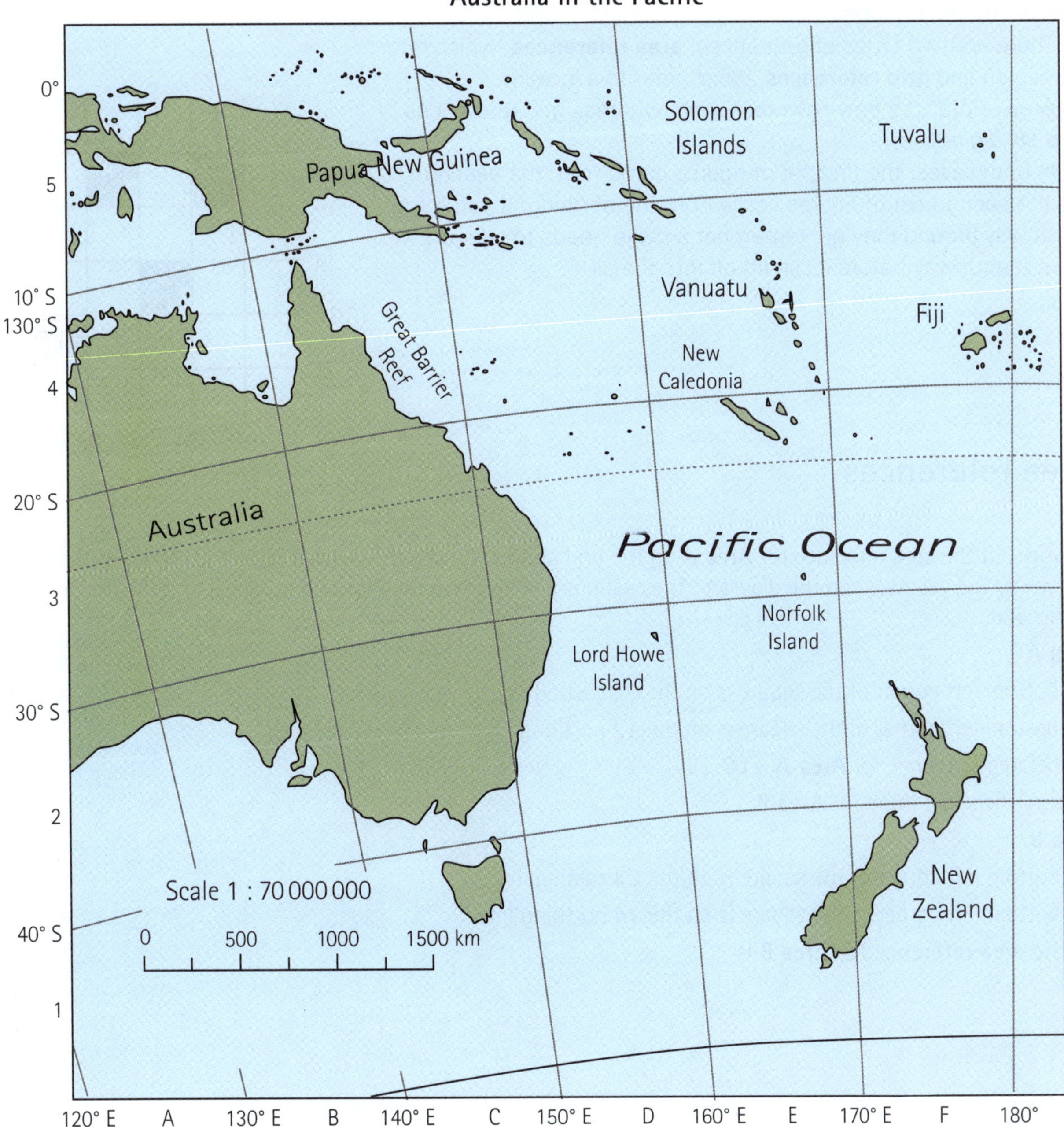

UNIT 19
GRID REFERENCES

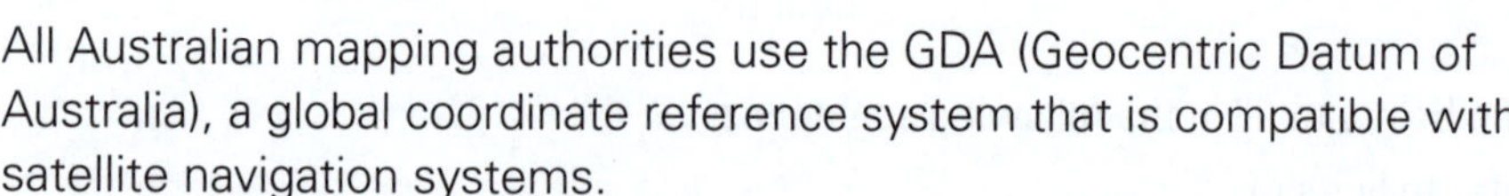

All Australian mapping authorities use the GDA (Geocentric Datum of Australia), a global coordinate reference system that is compatible with satellite navigation systems.

A grid on a map is a set of parallel lines that run vertically and horizontally. They are separate from latitude and longitude lines.

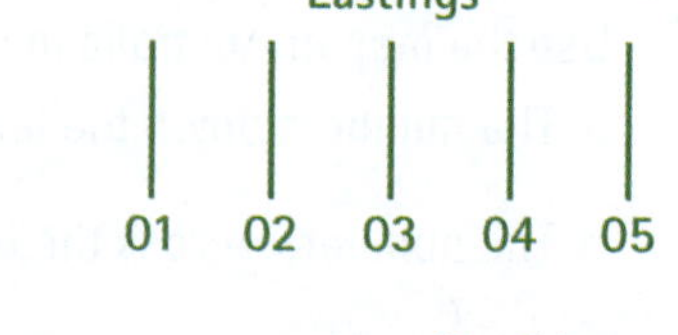

The vertical grid lines run up and down the map and are numbered to the east (from left to right, west to east) so are called **eastings**.

The horizontal lines run from side to side and are numbered to the north (from bottom to top, south to north) so are called **northings**.

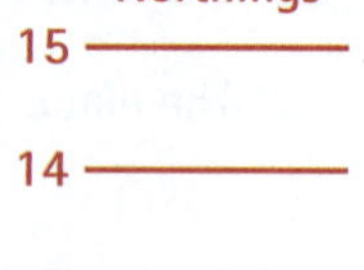

Grid lines are numbered so you can look up the grid references for a place and use them to find the place quickly.

Together, eastings and northings make a grid pattern as in the example on the right below.

There are two types of references: **area references**, which refer to a region and **grid references**, which refer to a location.

Area references only have *four digits* whereas grid references have *six digits*.

In both cases, the first set of figures come from the easting and the second set of figures come from the northing. If you forget which way around they go, remember a plane needs to take off down the runway before it can lift off into the air.

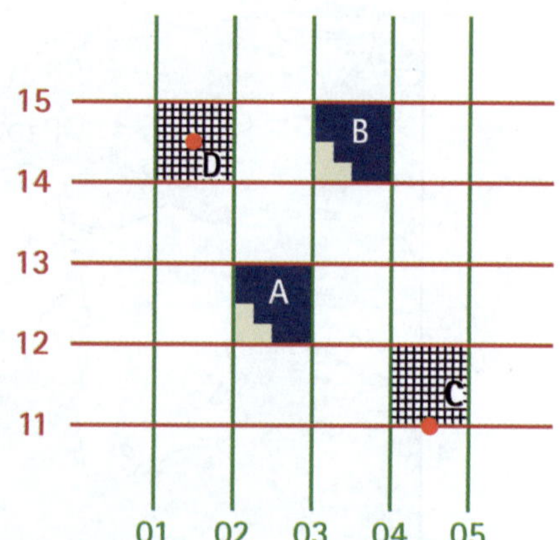

Area references

To work out the area reference for **Area A** on the grid above, you use the bottom left hand corner of the area (shown by the yellow on the diagram) The eastings will give you the first two numbers and the northings the second.

Area A

The bottom left corner of the square is on the 02 easting line

The bottom left corner of the square is on the 12 northing line

So the area reference for **Area A** is 02 12

Let's try the same thing for **Area B**

Area B

The bottom left corner of the square is on the 03 easting line

The bottom left corner of the square is on the 14 northing line

So the area reference for Area B is ______________.

ISBN 9780170367073

Grid references

Remember, grid references have *six figures:* the **first** three are the easting and the **second** three are the northing. To work out the grid reference for Point C you first need to work out what square the dot is located in.

Point C is in the square 04 11.

You then need to say where in the square the dot is located. Each square is separated into tenths, just like centimetres on a ruler.

Point C is halfway between 04 and 05 on the eastings line, which means it is on 5, so the easting reading is 045.

Point C is directly on the 11 line; to say that we put a 0, so the northing reading is 110.

So the grid reference for Point C is 045 110

Let's try the same thing for Point D

Point D

The point is located in the square 01 14

The point is located halfway between 01 and 02 so that is 5

The point is located halfway between 14 and 15 so that is 5

The grid reference for Point D is ______________.

1 Give the area references for the following symbols.

☺ ______________

💧 ______________

❄ ______________

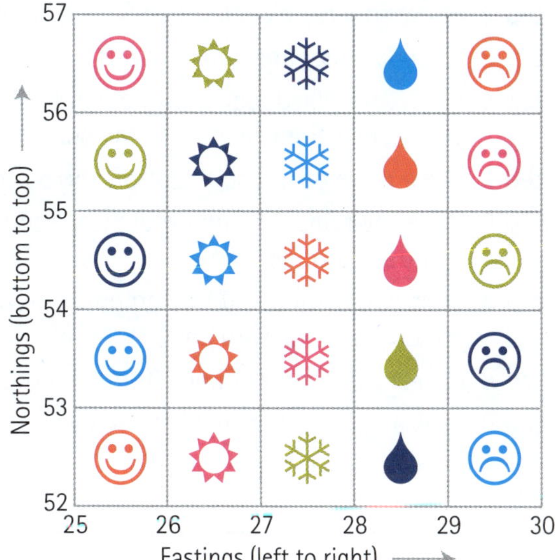

2 Beside each X on the map on the right, write the name of the feature the X refers to. Work out the answers by using the following grid references.

045140 = beacon

042110 = berry gardens

044115 = cool storage sheds

014115 = airstrip

025124 = cemetery

033128 = solar panels

020140 = tennis centre

028145 = historic monument

015134 = heliport

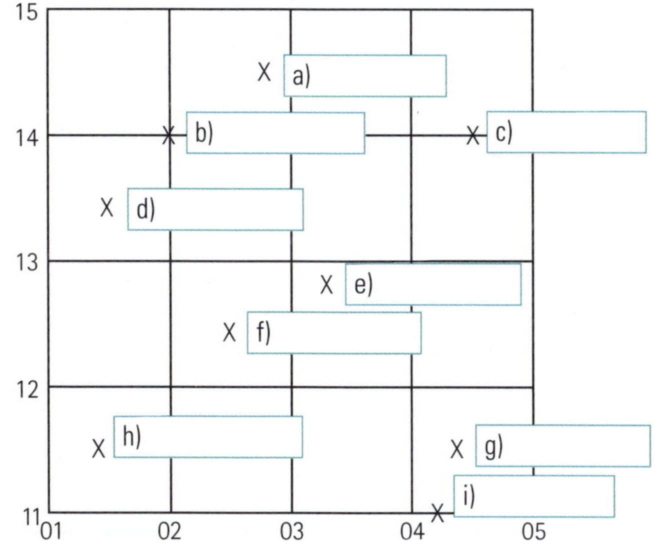

ISBN 9780170367073

UNIT 20

CONTOUR LINES

Contour lines show you the shape and height of the land, or the **relief**. You can easily show a house or a road on a map from a bird's-eye view by using lines and squares, but it is not as easy to show the hills and valleys.

The best way to show where areas change height and shape is by using contour lines. A contour line joins places of equal height in the same way that isobars on a weather map join areas of equal pressure.

Playdough mountains

To get an idea of the connection between what hills look like from the side and what they will look like on a contour map, carry out the following activity.

You will need a small tub of playdough or plasticine, a ruler, a grey lead pencil and some cotton thread or fishing line.

Step 1: Build your own mountain using the playdough.

Step 2: In the square below labelled Sketch, draw a sketch of your mountain.

Step 3: Use your ruler and pencil to put a dot every centimetre up the side of your mountain.

Step 4: Place your playdough mountain in the box labelled Contour and trace around the bottom of it using your pencil. Remove it from the box.

Step 5: Use a piece of thread to cut off the bottom section of the mountain at the 1 cm mark.

Step 6: Place the remaining mountain (top section) in the centre of the previous contour line in the Contour box and trace around it again

Step 7: Continue cutting and tracing until you have mapped the mountain. Mark the peak of your mountain in the Contour box with an X.

Step 8: Number the contour lines from 1 on the bottom to as many as you need to the top line.

Step 9: Look at the relationship between your original sketch and the contour line diagram.

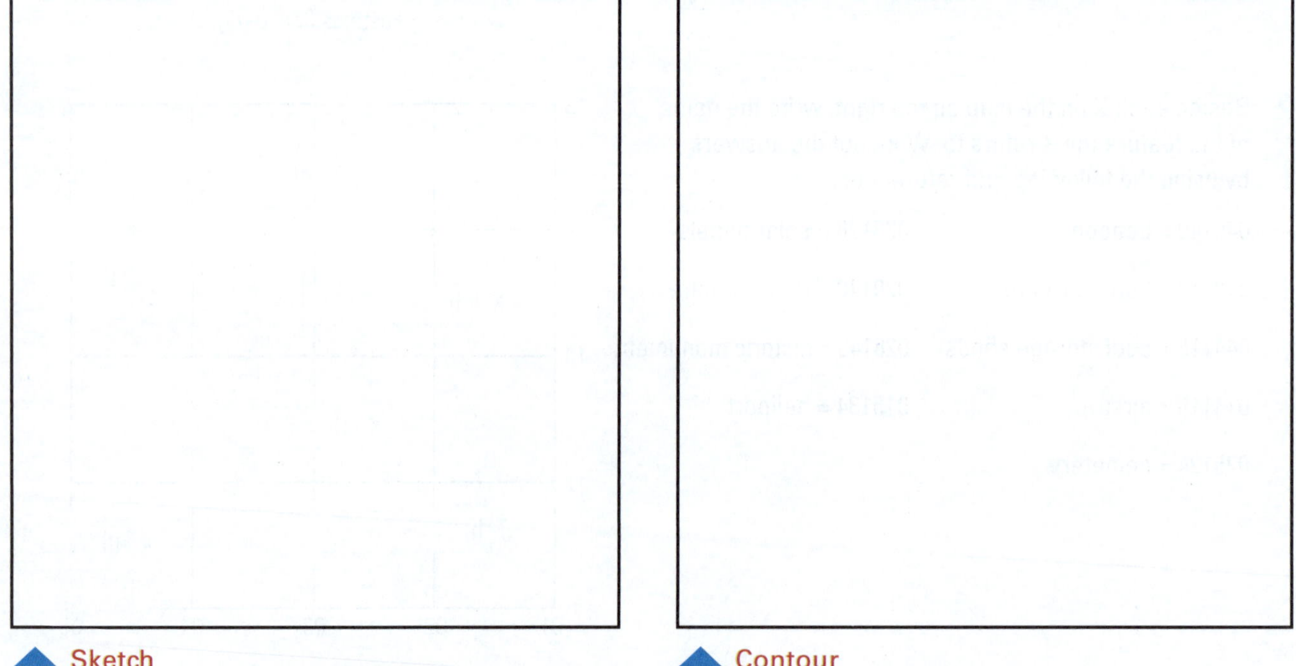

Sketch

Contour

ISBN 9780170367073

Contour lines on a map will look like this.

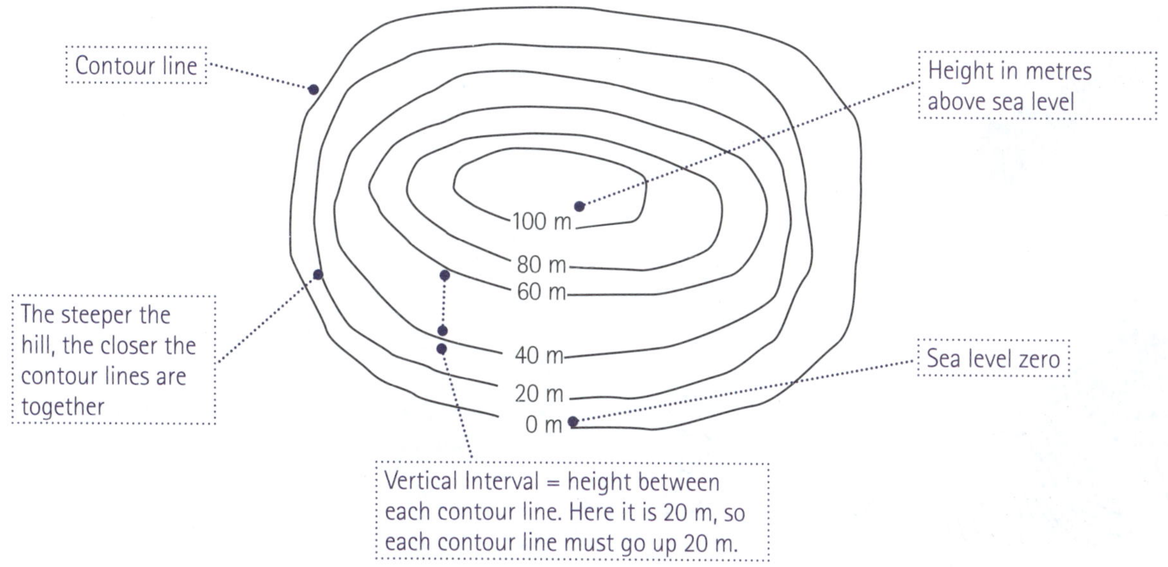

Contour lines of common features

Landforms that will be seen on a topographic map

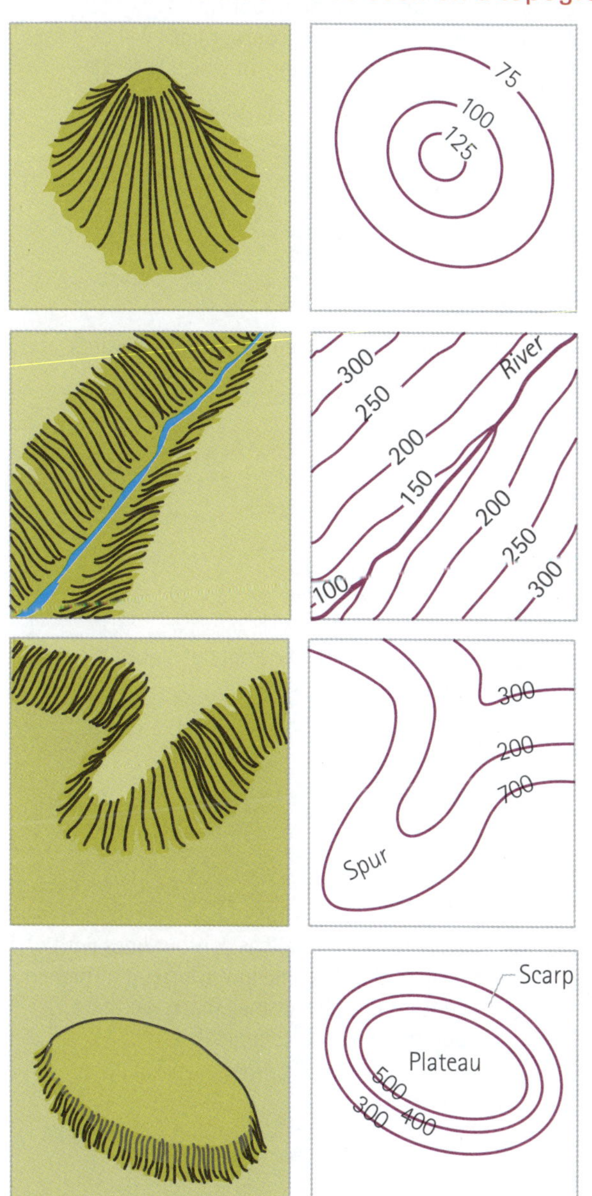

Hill

An area of land that is higher than the surrounding area. It is not high enough to be called a mountain.

Valley

A long and usually narrow indentation in the Earth's surface. Most valleys have rivers running through them.

Spur

A finger of highland. Often valleys are separated by spurs.

Plateau

An elevated area of fairly level land. It is often bounded by steep land known as a *scarp*.

ISBN 9780170367073

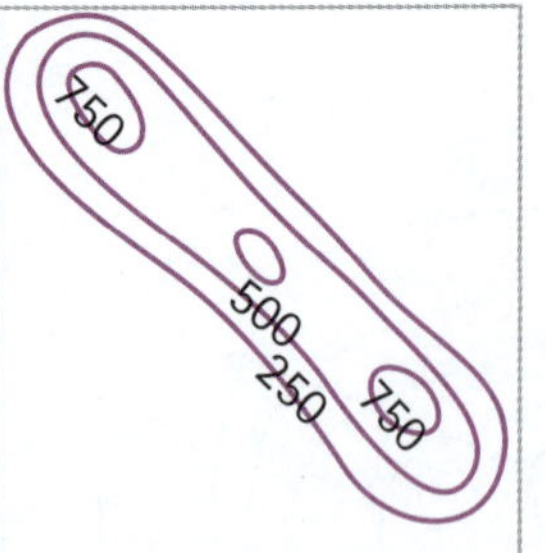

Ridge

A long, narrow area of high land, steeply sloped on either side.

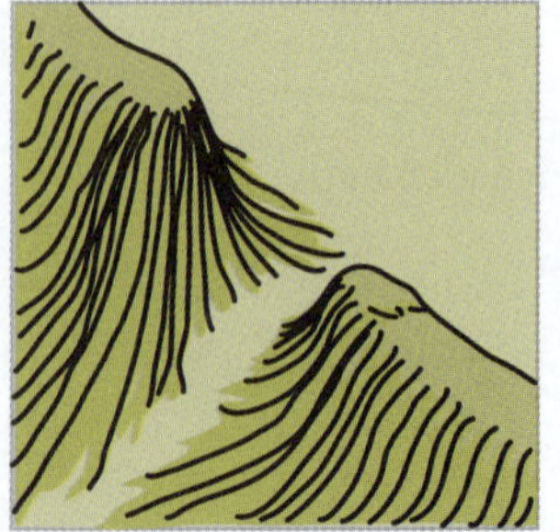
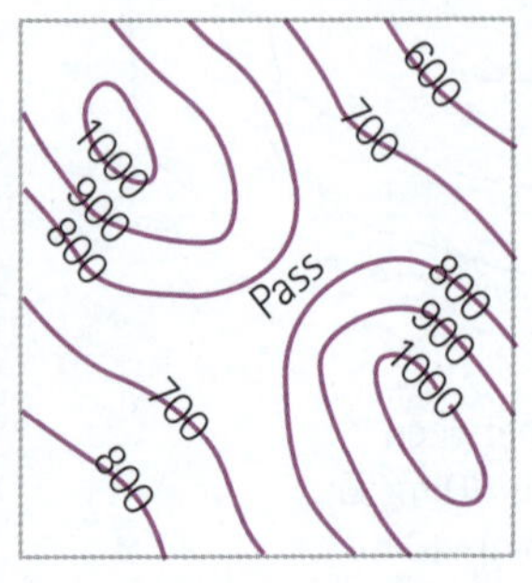

Pass

A lower area between two highland areas. Often these are used as transport routes.

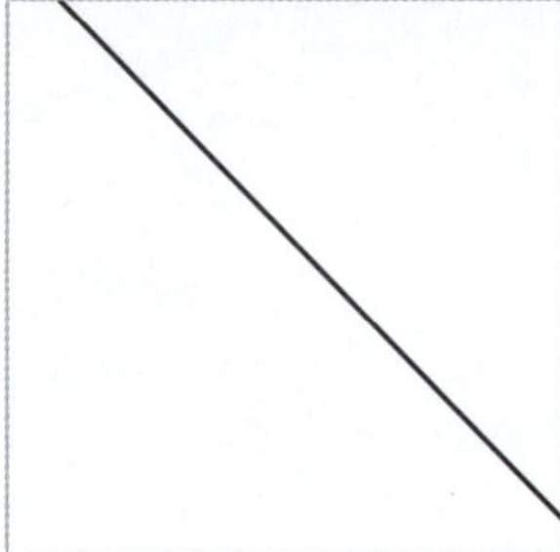
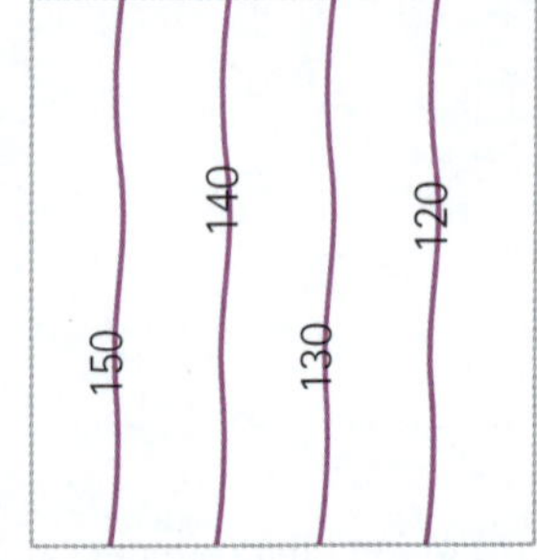

Uniform slope

A slope that is constant from top to bottom. It may be steeply sloping, in which case the contour lines will be close together, or it may be gently sloping, in which case the contours will be widely spaced.

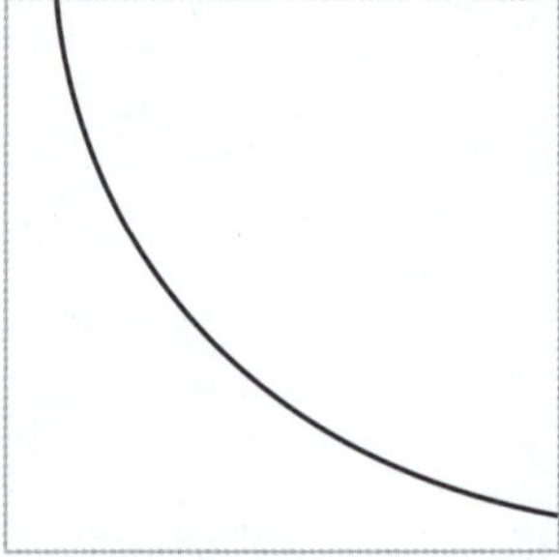
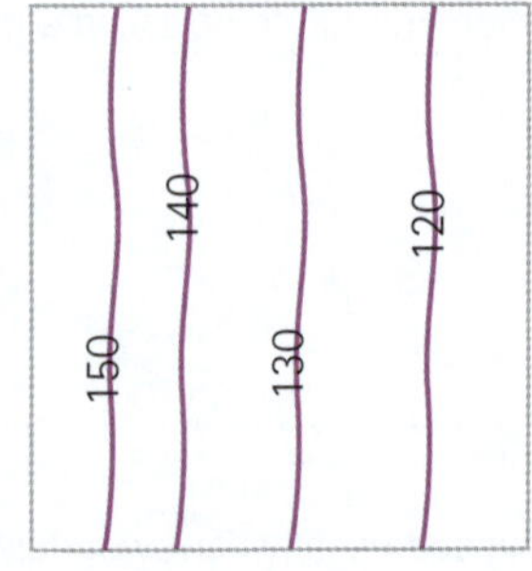

Concave slope

A slope that is gentle at the bottom but steeper towards the top.

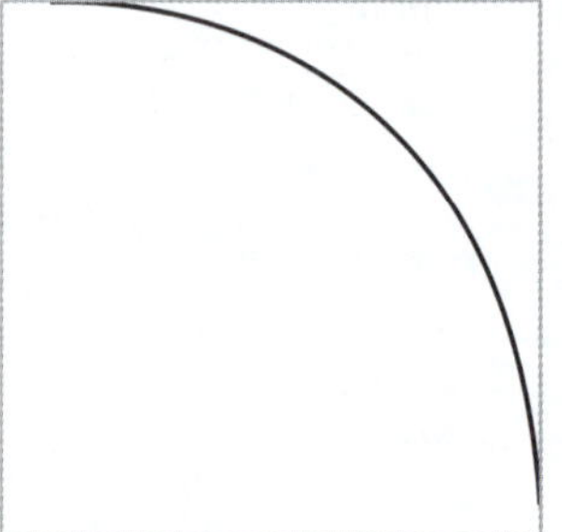
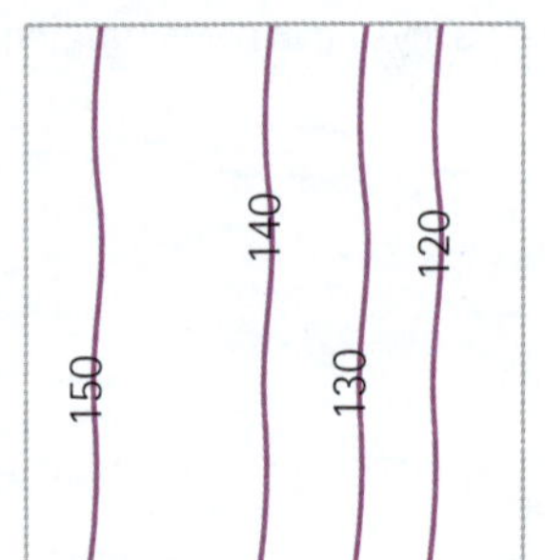

Convex slope

A slope that is steep towards the bottom but slopes more gently towards the top.

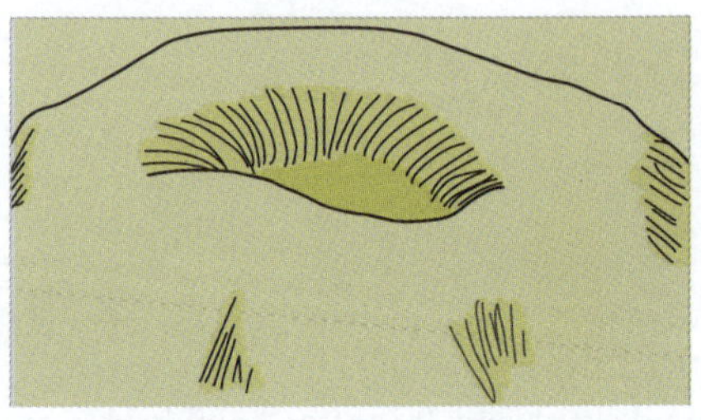
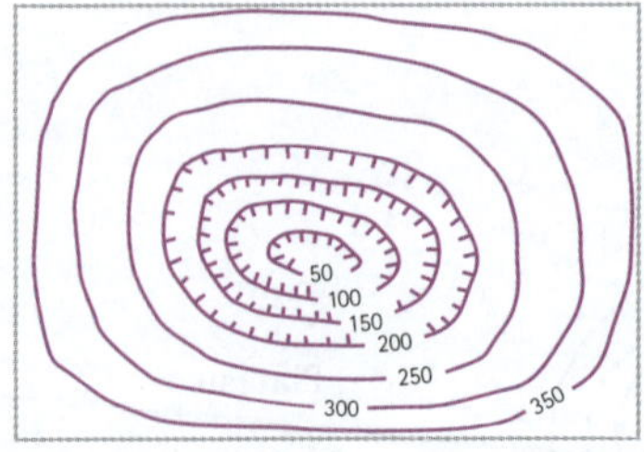

Depression

A depression (hole) has contour lines with heights that become lower instead of higher; contour lines have small marks on them pointing towards the middle.

ISBN 9780170367073

1 Give the heights of the points marked from a to f.

a ____________

b ____________

c ____________

d ____________

e ____________

f ____________

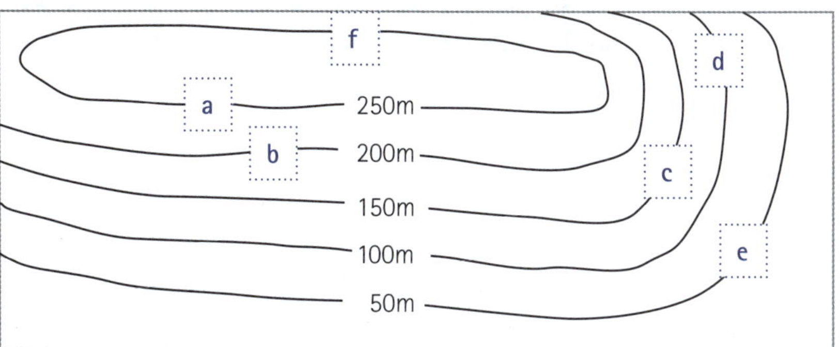

2 Write down the name of the feature shown by the contour lines.

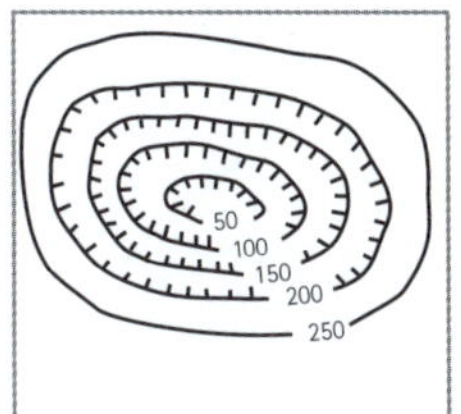

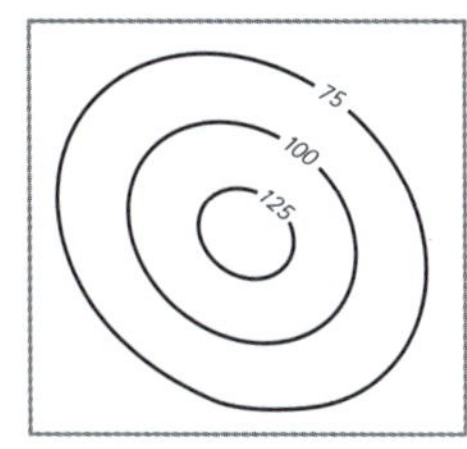

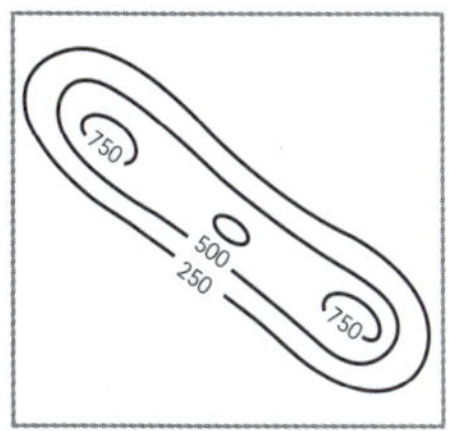

a ____________ b ____________ c ____________

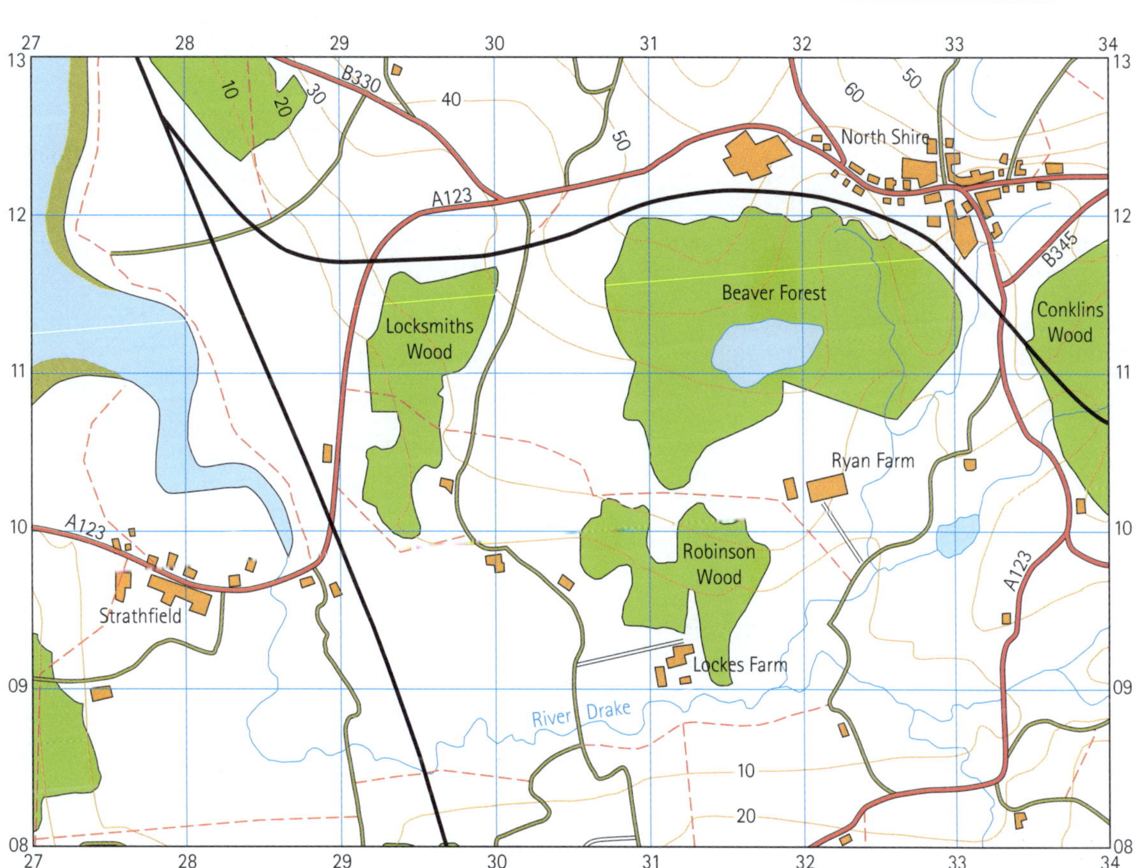

3 Using the map above, answer the following questions.

a Name a human feature. ____________

b Name a natural feature. ____________

c What colour are the rivers? ____________

d The lines that show the height about sea level are called ____________.

e Circle the correct answer. The land on this map is steep / not steep.

ISBN 9780170367073

UNIT 21
CROSS-SECTIONS

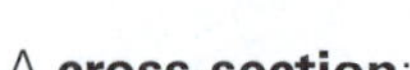

A **cross-section**:

- begins with a map and ends up a graph
- is made using contour lines
- gives a picture of relief – where land goes up and down
- is called a cross-section because it shows what the land looks like along one line, as if a giant knife has cut through the land, scraped away one half and has left you looking at the side of the half that remains.

How to draw a cross-section

Aim: To draw a cross-section of the island along the A–B line.

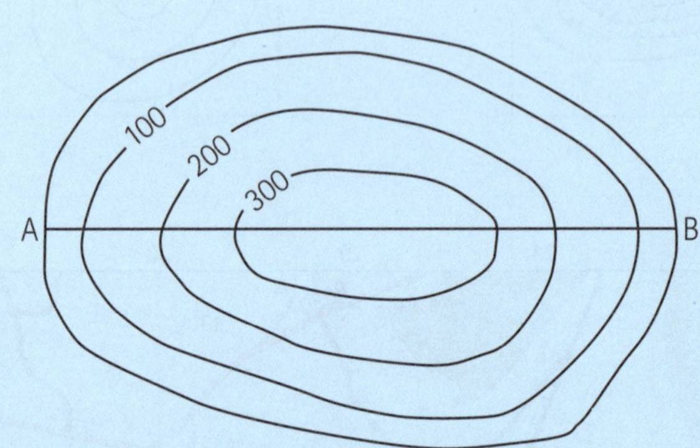

1. Put the straight edge of a piece of paper along the line.
2. Each time a contour line crosses the paper, mark the paper with a line and the height.

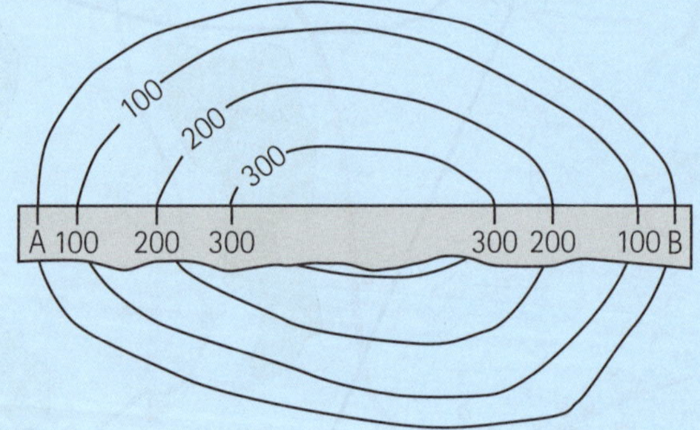

3. Draw a vertical and horizontal axis for a graph.
4. The horizontal axis (*x*-axis) should be the width of the cross-section.
5. Label the vertical axis (*y*-axis) in metres. One centimetre represents one metre.
6. Put your piece of paper with contour lines along the *x*-axis.
7. Move the paper up 1 centimetre at a time and put crosses on the graph to match the marks for that height.
8. Continue to move up the graph 1 centimetre at a time, putting crosses in the correct places.
9. Remove the paper and join the crosses with a smooth line.
10. Label the beginning and end of your cross-section on the *x*-axis.

This is your cross-section.

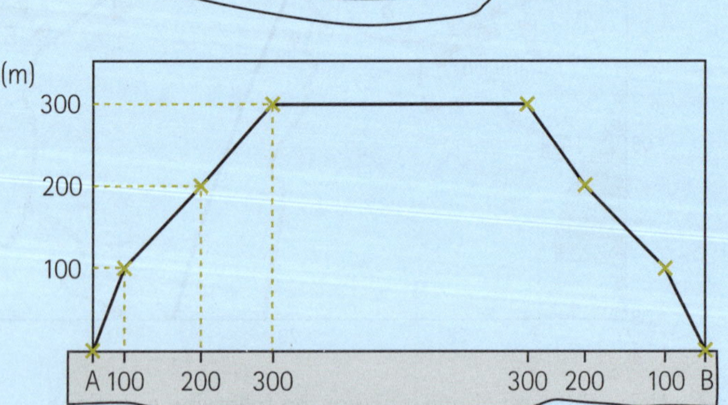

ISBN 9780170367073

1 Label the following cross-sections as mountain, valley, plain or plateau.

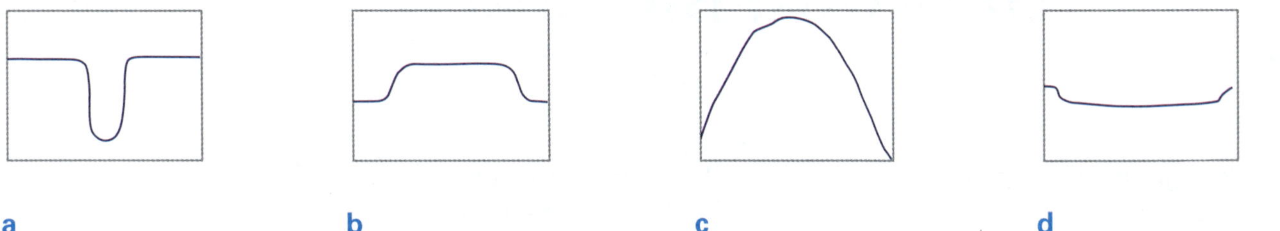

a ______________ b ______________ c ______________ d ______________

2 a Get a scrap piece of paper with a straight edge and mark in the heights along the piece of paper that are needed to draw a cross-section.

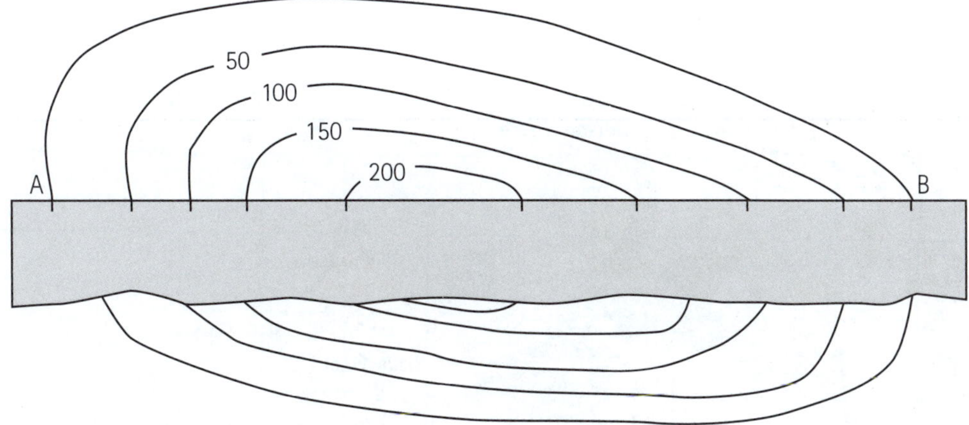

b Label the horizontal and vertical axes on the graph frame below and use the marks on the scrap paper to draw your cross-section.

ISBN 9780170367073

UNIT 22
TOPOGRAPHIC MAPS

Topography (say t'**pog**-ra-fee) comes from the Greek words *topos*, meaning 'place', and *graphy* meaning 'to write'. It means detailed drawing describing the geographical features of a place.

A **topographic map** is about the land. It shows the features on the land.

Features can be human or natural features.

human features = made by people, such as roads

natural features = made by nature, such as rivers

Mackay

Map created by Geospatial Analysis & Mapping Branch, National Title Tribunal. Topographic image data © Commonwealth of Australia, used under licence from Geoscience Australia.

 ISBN 9780170367073

1 Separate the list below into human features and natural features by highlighting the natural features in green and the human features in yellow.

street	reef	sea
water tower	reservoir	creek
beach	water supply installation	mangroves
causeway	airport	golf course
bay	cemetery	hospital
bridge	port	

2 Use the map of Mackay opposite to answer the following questions.

a The blue area near the airport is a ______________________________.

b Name one human feature on the map that is not in the list above. ______________________________

c Name a natural feature on the map that is not in the list above. ______________________________

d The black broken lines show ______________________________.

e What do you think gauge 2'0" refers to? ______________________________

f Would it flood here very often? Give a reason for your answer. ______________________________

g What direction is Mount Oscar from Bassett Basin? ______________________________

h What direction is Dangerous Reef from Slade Islet? ______________________________

i How long is the runway that runs SW to NE at the airport? ______________________________

j How far is it by train from Mackay to Maraju? ______________________________

k What is the area reference (four figures) for Slade Bay? ______________________________

l What is the area reference (four figures) for Mackay West? ______________________________

m What feature is found at each of the following grid references?

330 581 ______________________________

244 665 ______________________________

259 601 ______________________________

n Give the grid reference (six figures) for the following features:

Mt Bassett ______________________________

Hospital ______________________________

Racecourse ______________________________

UNIT 23
PRECIS MAPS

The *four rules* about drawing a precis map are:

1 Work out exactly what you need to show and what to leave out.
2 Make it simple.
3 Make it neat.
4 Make it big and clear.

> The word **precis** (say **pray**-see) comes from French.
> ▲ **precis** = summary; picking out the main points
> ▲ **precis map** = summary of another map; showing the main points

How to draw a precis map

To draw a precis map:

- ▲ give your map a title
- ▲ draw a border in the same proportions as the actual map (use a ruler)
- ▲ draw any coastline, large rivers and main roads (these don't need to show every bend, just the general shape)
- ▲ draw in the required features
- ▲ name the features on the map and make a legend/key
- ▲ give the map a scale if possible
- ▲ give the map a north point/orientation.

1 **Put your own colour on the precis map of Mackay and make the legend/key match the colours you have chosen.**

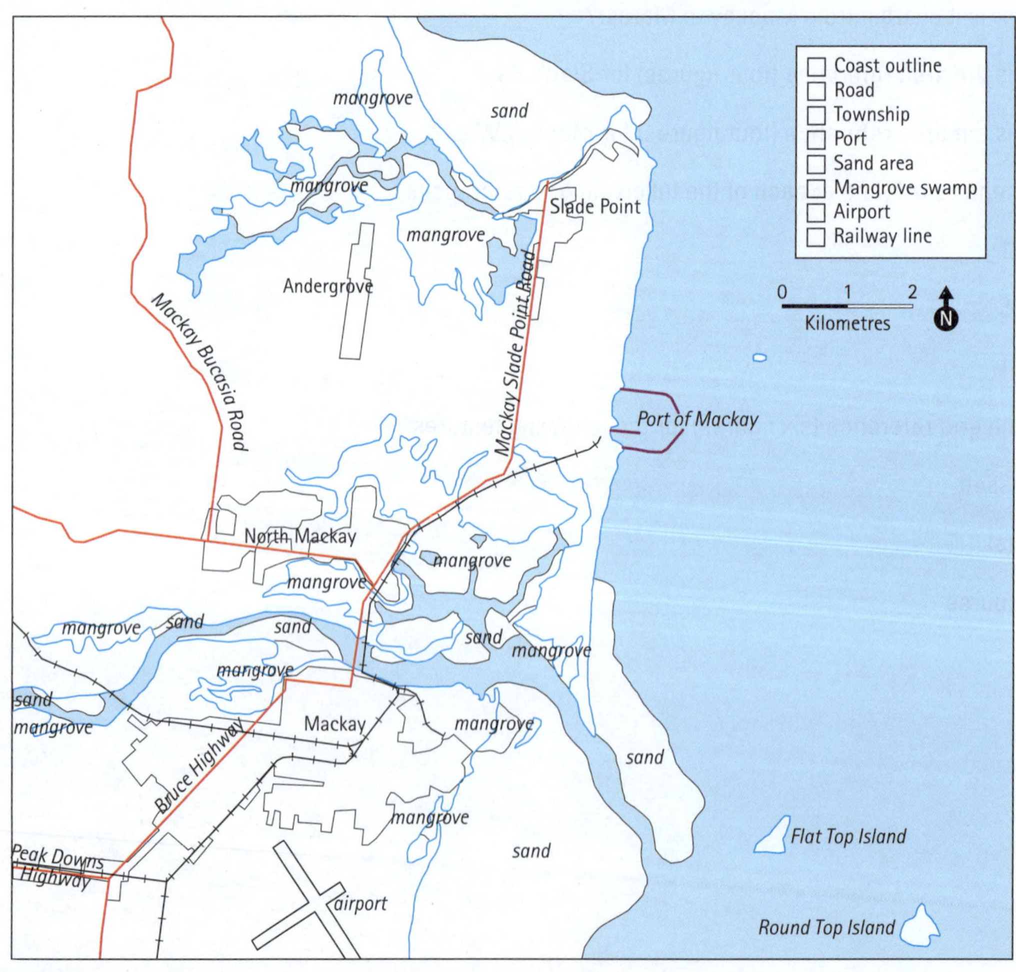

▲ Precis map of Mackay drawn from the map in Unit 22

 ISBN 9780170367073

2 Li was asked to find the following features on a map and to put them onto a precis map. Colour the features on Li's precis map.

- ▲ pine plantation (light green tree symbols)
- ▲ township (pink)
- ▲ scrub (scrub symbol on light green background)
- ▲ road (red)
- ▲ orchards (green dots)
- ▲ river (blue)

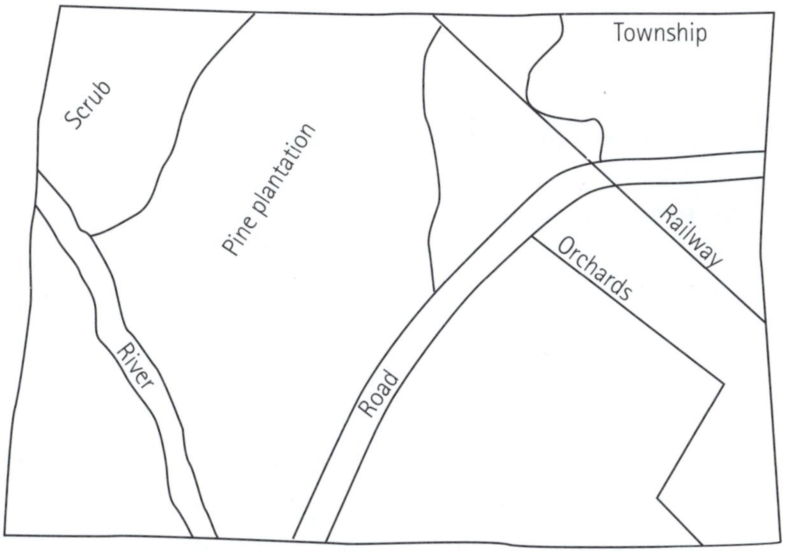

3 Li has located and placed all the features correctly on his map but made five mistakes with his map. List the mistakes.

a ______________________________

b ______________________________

c ______________________________

d ______________________________

e ______________________________

4 Use the cultural features aerial photograph on page 51 to produce a precis sketch showing the green space, housing developments, industry, roads and railways.

ISBN 9780170367073

UNIT 24
AERIAL PHOTOGRAPHS

Aerial photographs are taken from the air. They can be taken from one of two angles:

1. **Vertical angle** = bird's-eye view or directly overhead; it is often harder to identify things in the photograph from this angle. You can work out the scale of the photograph by using a map of the same area.
2. **Oblique angle** = taken from an angle. Oblique means sloping rather than direct, making it easier to pick out the various features in the photograph. The scale at the foreground and background of the photograph will be different.

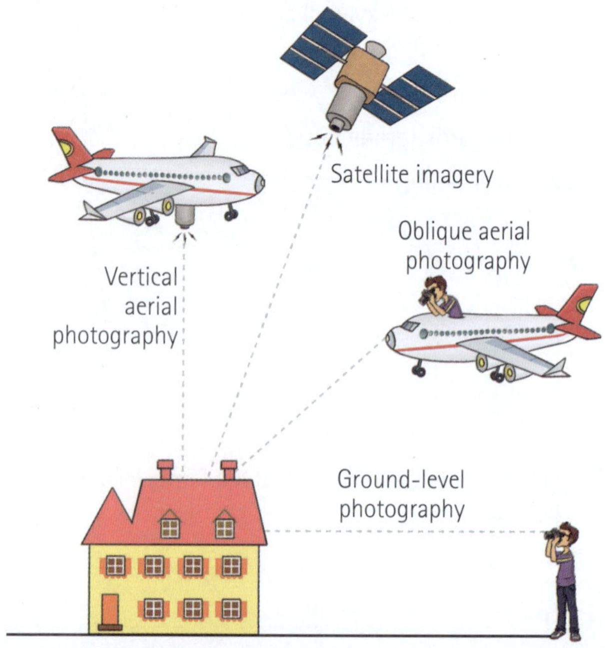

What features often look like from the air

Natural features

Bending, uneven, random pattern

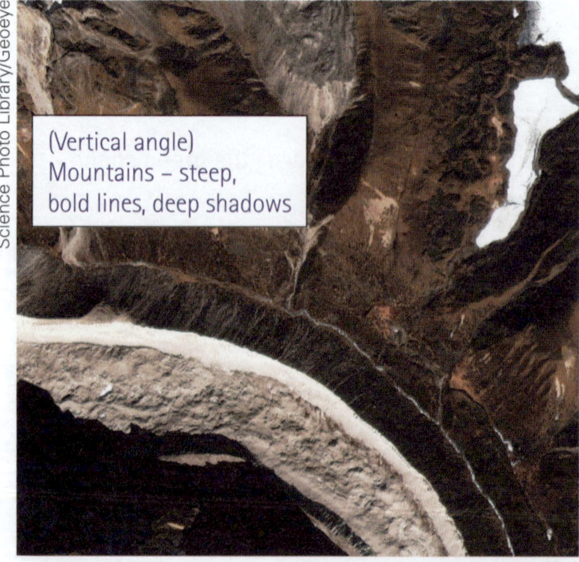

Science Photo Library/Geoeye

Science Photo Library/Alexis Rosenfeld

Alamy/LOOK Die Bildagentur der Fotografen GmbH

Alamy/Anthony Dunn

ISBN 9780170367073

Cultural features

Straight, parallel, geometric, regular pattern

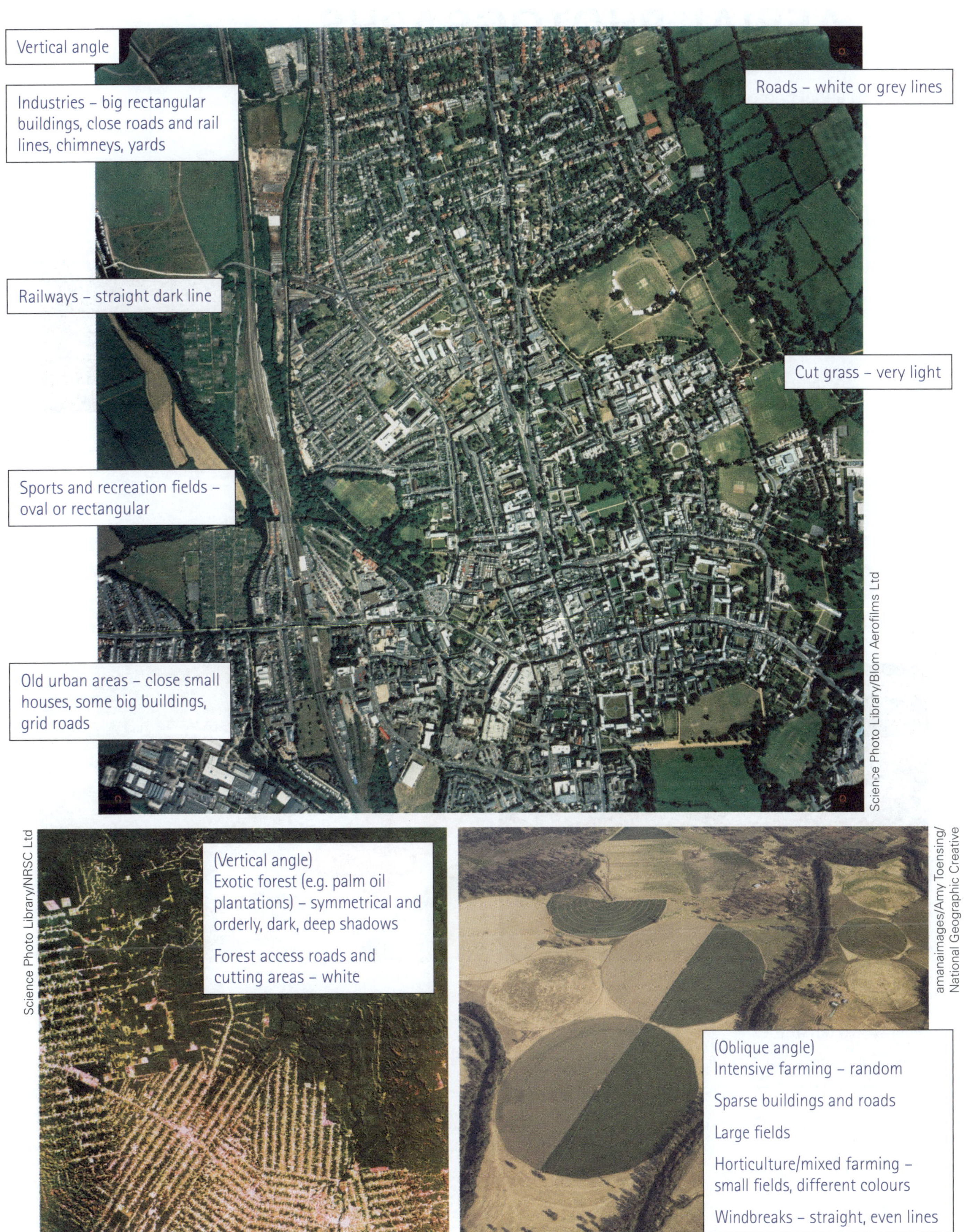

1 For each of the aerial photographs in this unit, draw an arrow connecting one of the features in the text box to an example on the photograph.

ISBN 9780170367073

UNIT 25
PRECIS SKETCHES FROM AERIAL PHOTOGRAPHS

A vertical aerial photograph is taken looking straight down. So a precis sketch from a vertical aerial photograph can be sketched inside an ordinary square or rectangle.

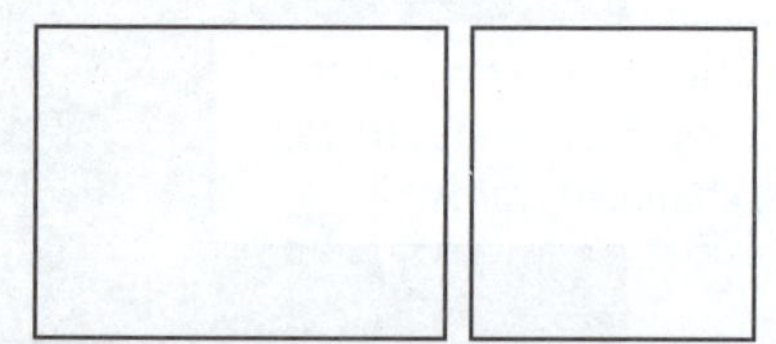

An oblique aerial photograph is taken on an angle. The distance from A to B is shorter than the distance from C to D because of the angle from which the photograph was taken.

Alamy/Andrew Holt

So a precis sketch from an oblique photograph has to be sketched inside a trapezium frame.

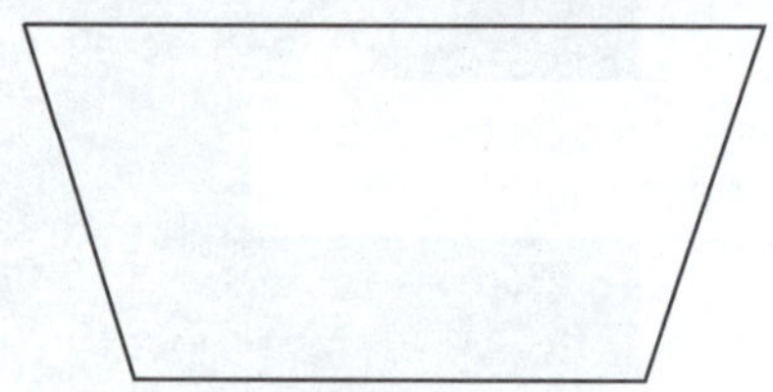

Making a precis sketch from an aerial photograph

Shutterstock.com/B Brown

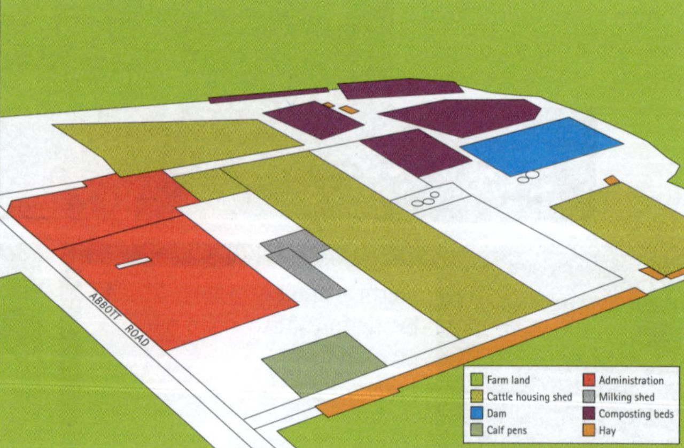

- Give the sketch a title
- Draw the frame – square, rectangle or trapezium shape
- Draw the outline of any coastline or water or regions
- Draw features as shaded areas – e.g. instead of drawing individual green houses on a farm, draw the boundary around them
- Give the sketch a legend/key
- Where possible, include a scale

ISBN 9780170367073

1 Use the aerial photograph below to create a precis sketch of the area. The water courses have already been marked on the sketch for you.

Alamy/Bill Bachman

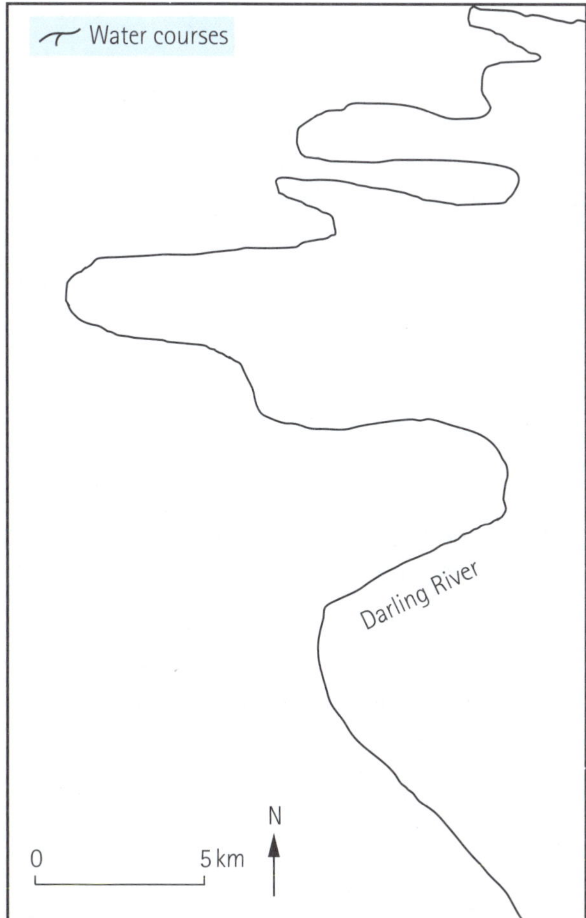

- Mark the roads, paddocks and township on your precis sketch.
- Make sure the extra symbols you create are added to your legend.
- Give the sketch a title.
- Add two textboxes: in the first, describe the course of the main river and what its banks look like.
- In the second textbox, describe a relationship between the location of paddocks and the location of water courses.

Scribble Maps is a website that allows you to use Google Maps and Google Maps satellite images to create your own precis sketches by drawing over the top of the background image. You can search for locations and highlight features that are important for your discussion.

UNIT 26
DESCRIBING PATTERNS

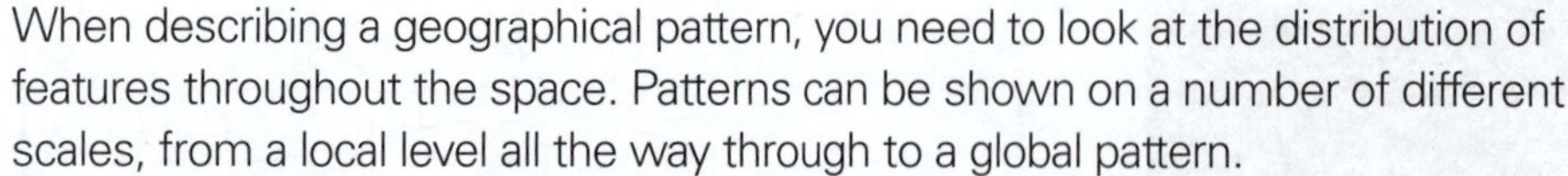

When describing a geographical pattern, you need to look at the distribution of features throughout the space. Patterns can be shown on a number of different scales, from a local level all the way through to a global pattern.

A pattern can describe many different factors, such as:

- ▲ Human – the location of roads and train networks
- ▲ Land – where earthquakes occur
- ▲ Air – how a cyclone moves
- ▲ Water – the impact of flooding along a river

spatial (say **spay**–sh'l) = to do with spaces

data (say **dah-ta**) = values or facts collected from a primary or secondary source (singular is datum)

Geography is a spatial subject and involves looking at the patterns over space and the factors that may alter that pattern.

The easiest way to show a global pattern is to put (plot) the data on a map.

Once the data has been put on a map, you can start to see what sort of pattern is made.

The main types of patterns are:

Random pattern
Data has no clear design

Linear pattern
Data is in a line design

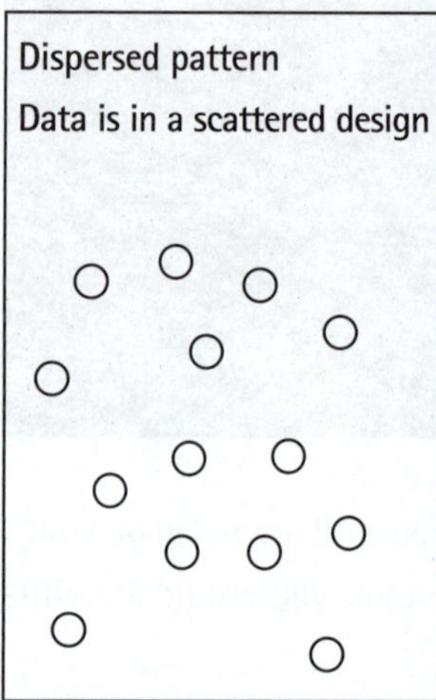

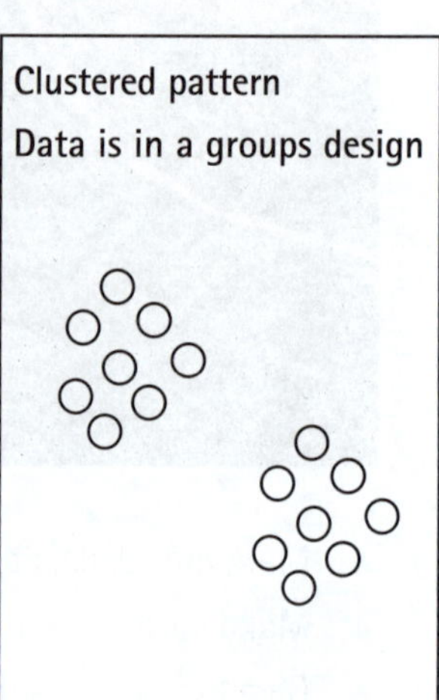

Whenever you are describing a pattern, use the PQE rule.

- ▲ **P**attern – What is the general pattern that you can see?
- ▲ **Q**uantify – Give an example of where you see that pattern and use values from the map where given
- ▲ **E**xception – Say where the pattern does not fit

1 State the type of distribution pattern for each of the boxes below and give examples of when this pattern might occur.

a Area A ______________________

b Area B ______________________

c Area C ______________________

Area A

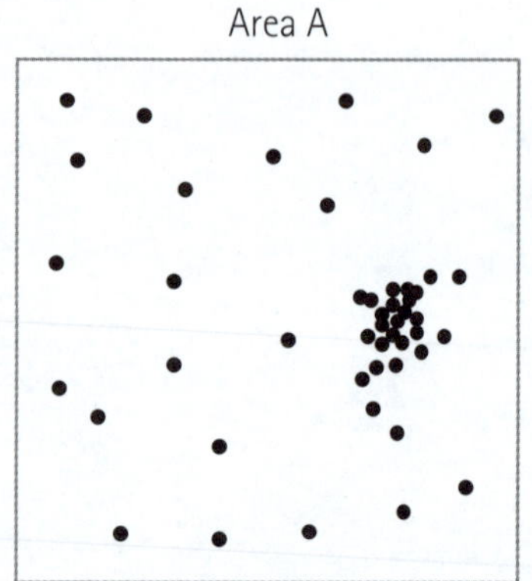

Area B

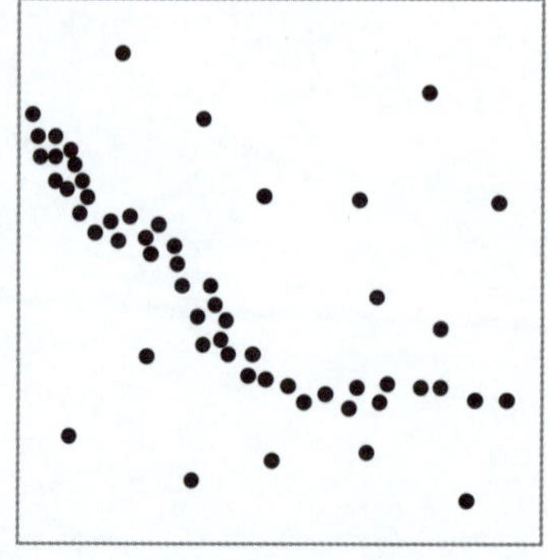

Area C

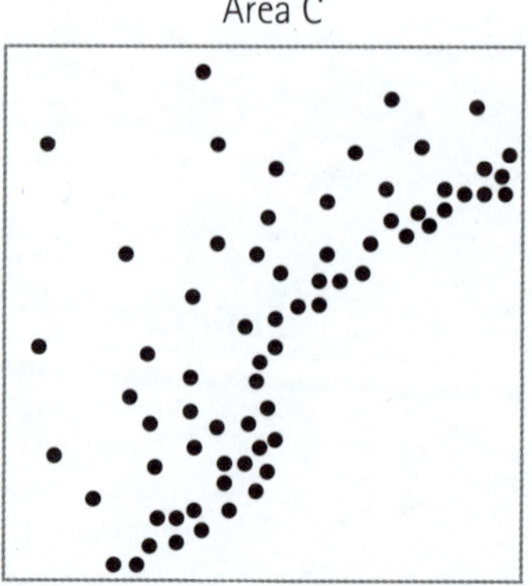

• One dot represents 200 people

ISBN 9780170367073

2 On the map of Australia, circle these patterns using the colours given.

a red circle = a linear pattern

b blue circle = random pattern

c green circle = dispersed pattern

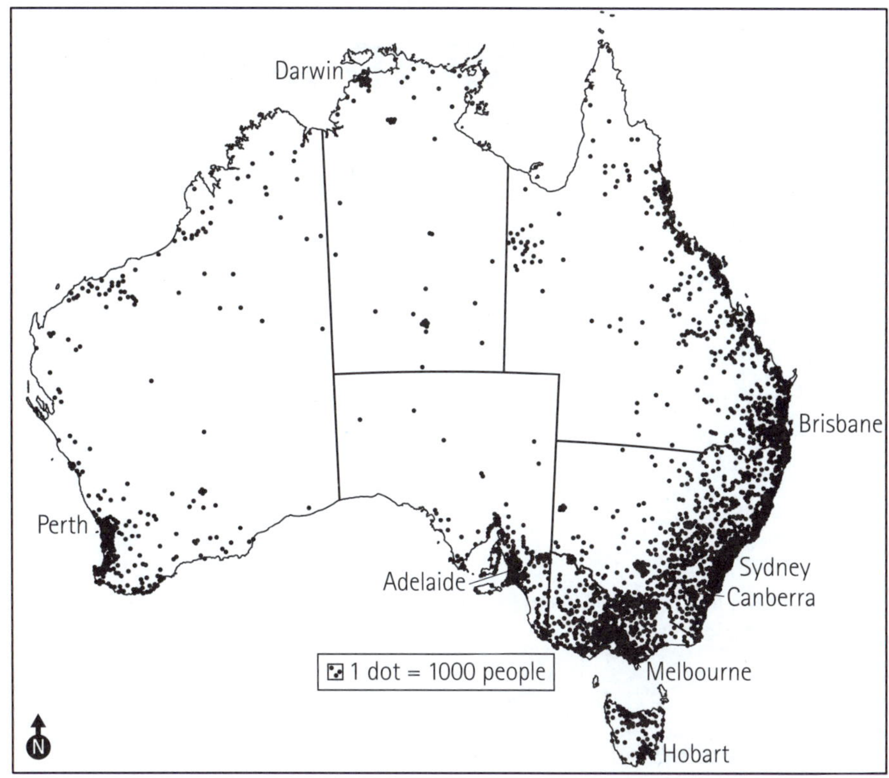

Source: Year Book Australia, 2008, (cat. No. 1301.0)

3 Fill in the gaps in the following sentences about the map below.

a The map below shows data about ______________________________.

b Its most obvious global pattern is ______________________________.

c An example of this would be ______________________________.

d An exception to this would be ______________________________.

e This map shows that out of Australia and New Zealand, people in ____________________ are more likely to be shaken out of bed in the morning.

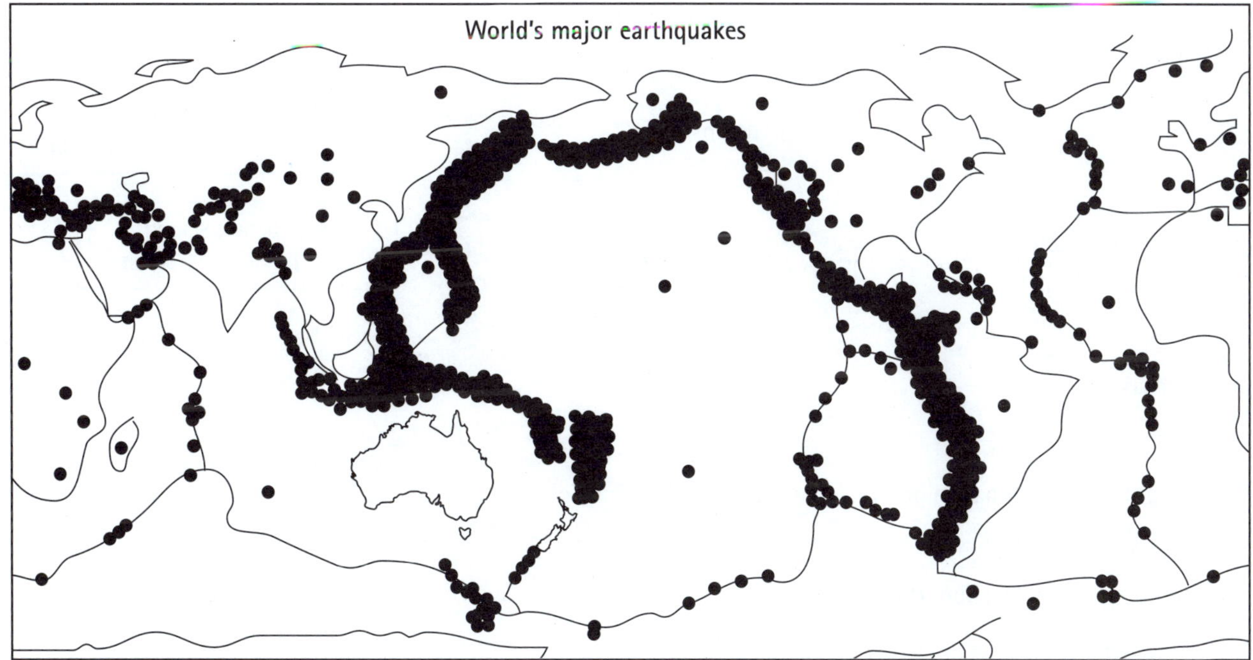

ISBN 9780170367073

UNIT 27
MIND MAPS

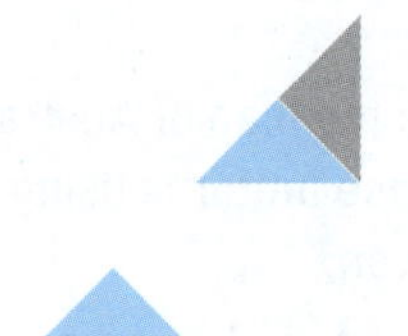

There are a number of different ways that you can create and structure a mind map. You need to see what works for you and what helps you the most. Here are some examples of the different ways you can present information to help you see relationships and remember things.

> **Mind map** = a visual summary
> Visual = showing by seeing
> Summary = leaving out unnecessary material and keeping only the necessary

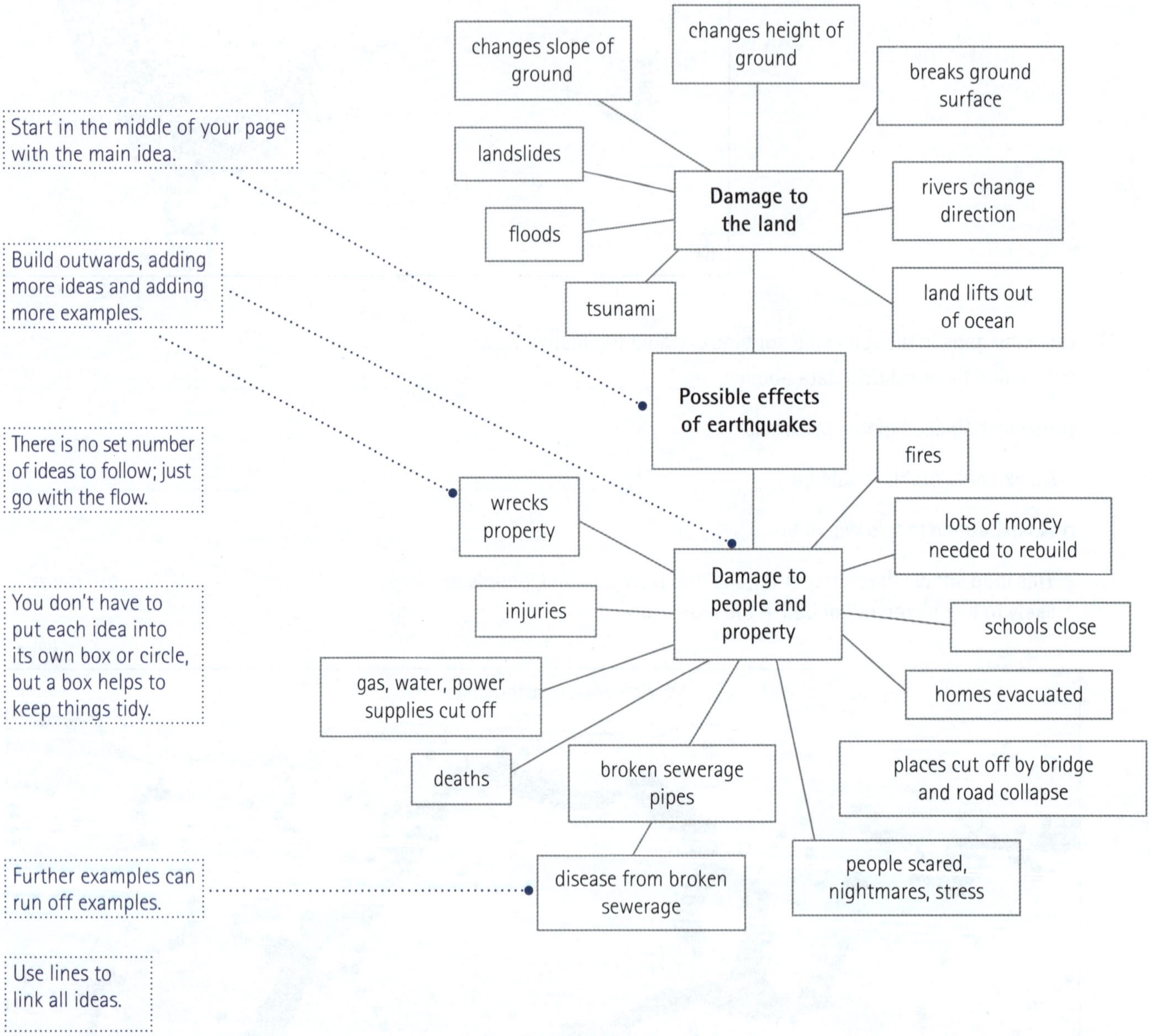

- **Possible effects of earthquakes**
  - **Damage to the land**
    - changes slope of ground
    - changes height of ground
    - breaks ground surface
    - landslides
    - rivers change direction
    - floods
    - tsunami
    - land lifts out of ocean
  - **Damage to people and property**
    - fires
    - wrecks property
    - lots of money needed to rebuild
    - injuries
    - schools close
    - homes evacuated
    - gas, water, power supplies cut off
    - deaths
    - broken sewerage pipes
      - disease from broken sewerage
    - places cut off by bridge and road collapse
    - people scared, nightmares, stress

Start in the middle of your page with the main idea.

Build outwards, adding more ideas and adding more examples.

There is no set number of ideas to follow; just go with the flow.

You don't have to put each idea into its own box or circle, but a box helps to keep things tidy.

Further examples can run off examples.

Use lines to link all ideas.

1 Colour the Rural–urban migration mind map on page 57 as follows:

Red = the main idea

Green = the two next important ideas

Yellow = the examples of those two ideas

Blue = the examples of an example

 ISBN 9780170367073

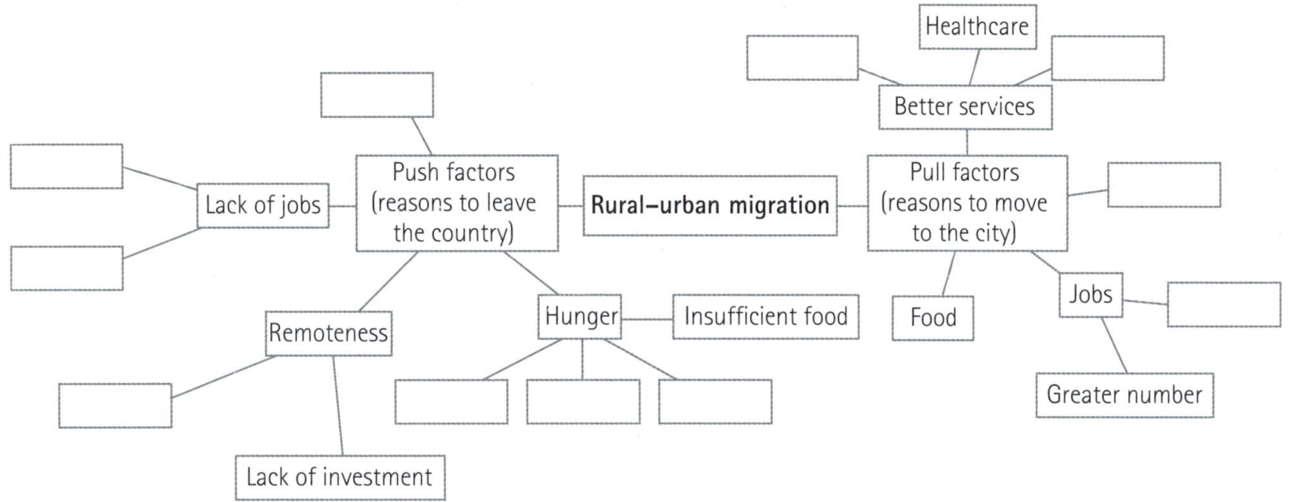

2 Decide whether the following are push factors or pull factors and add them to the mind map:

increasing mechanisation, drought, education, too many people, lack of services, housing, overgrazing, entertainment, poor soil, better pay, poor seed

3 Add a further example of better services.

In the study of migration, geographers identify two types of influences.

Push factor = reasons individuals have for leaving a location.

Pull factor = reasons that make the new location attractive.

Star diagrams

A **star diagram** is made using the idea of what a star in the sky looks like – a figure with several rays coming out in a regular order from a central point.

The star diagram has:

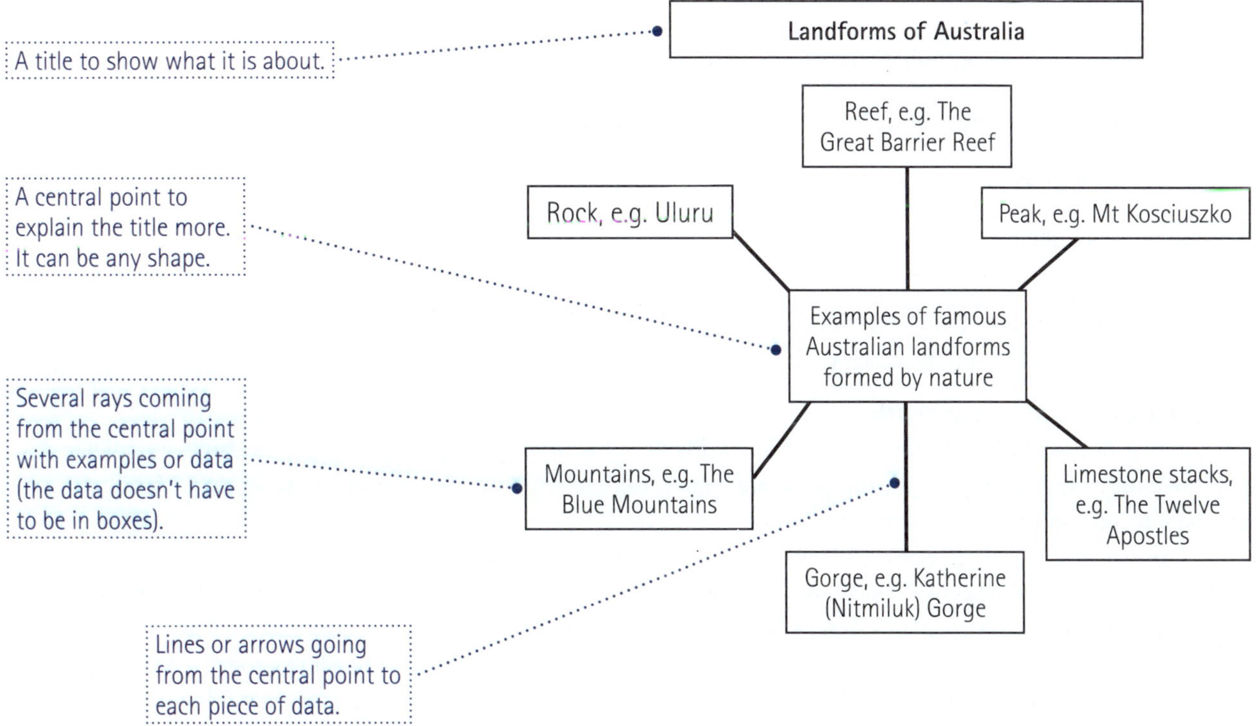

4 Colour the Landforms of Australia star diagram by using one colour for the title and the central point, and a different colour for the data.

ISBN 9780170367073

5 Sort the following data and use it to complete the star diagram below.

- ▲ Easy access to education
- ▲ Plenty of recycling and composting
- ▲ Sustainable cities
- ▲ High air quality
- ▲ Indicators that a place is sustainable
- ▲ Low working hours
- ▲ High renewable energy use
- ▲ Low vehicle kilometres travelled

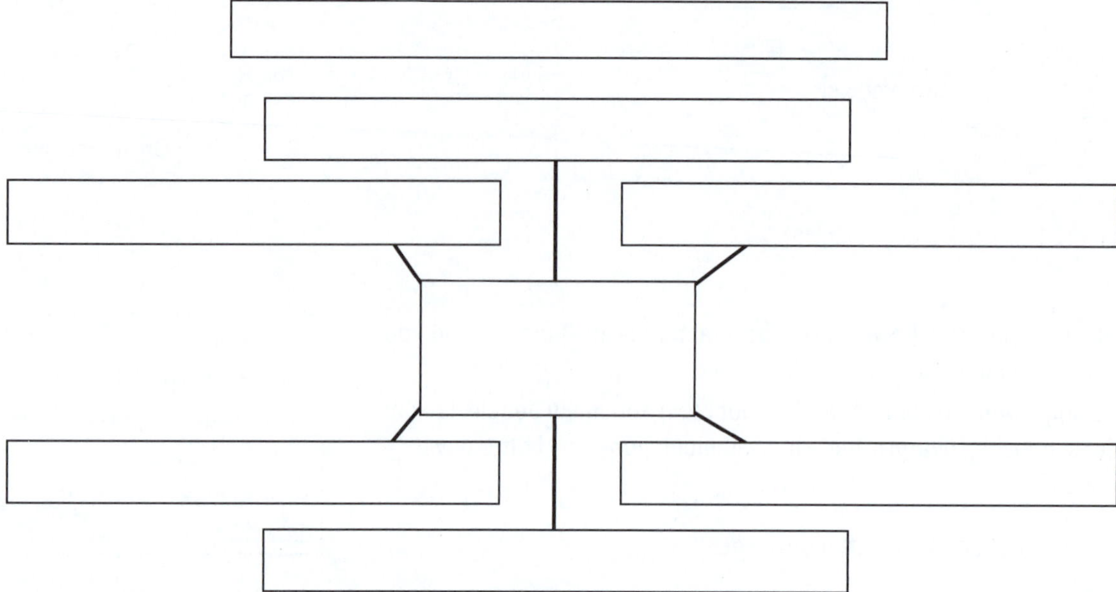

6 Read the following article and fill in the star diagram on the next page to show the main points, using information on the following topics. The heading has been done for you.

a The main point of the article

b Definition of 'megacity'

c Percentage of the world's inhabitants living in urban areas – 1950

d Estimated percentage of world's inhabitants living in urban areas – 2050

e Number of megacities in the world – 1950

f Number of megacities in the world – 2014

Geography in the news: The growth of megacities

By Neal Lineback and Mandy Lineback Gritzner

Megacities' expansive growth

For the first time in human history, more of the world's 6.8 billion people live in cities than in rural areas. That is an incredible demographic and geographic shift since 1950 when only 30 per cent of the world's 2.5 billion inhabitants lived in urban environments.

The world's largest cities, particularly in developing countries, are growing at phenomenal rates. As a growing landless class is attracted by urban opportunities, meagre as they might be, these cities' populations are ballooning to incredible numbers. A May 2010 *Christian Science Monitor* article on 'megacities' predicted that by 2050, almost 70 per cent of the world's estimated 10 billion people – more than the number of people living today – will reside in urban areas. The social, economic and environmental problems associated with a predominantly urbanised population are considerably different from those of the mostly rural world population of the past. A megacity is an urban agglomeration (accumulation) with more than 10 million inhabitants. Sixty years ago in 1950, there were only two megacities – New York-Newark and Tokyo. In 1995, 14 megacities existed. Today, there are 22, mostly in the developing countries of Asia, Africa and Latin America. By 2025, there will probably be 30 or more.

Geography in the News™ 17 February 2014 (Reprinted with permission of the authors, *Geography in the News*™)

 ISBN 9780170367073

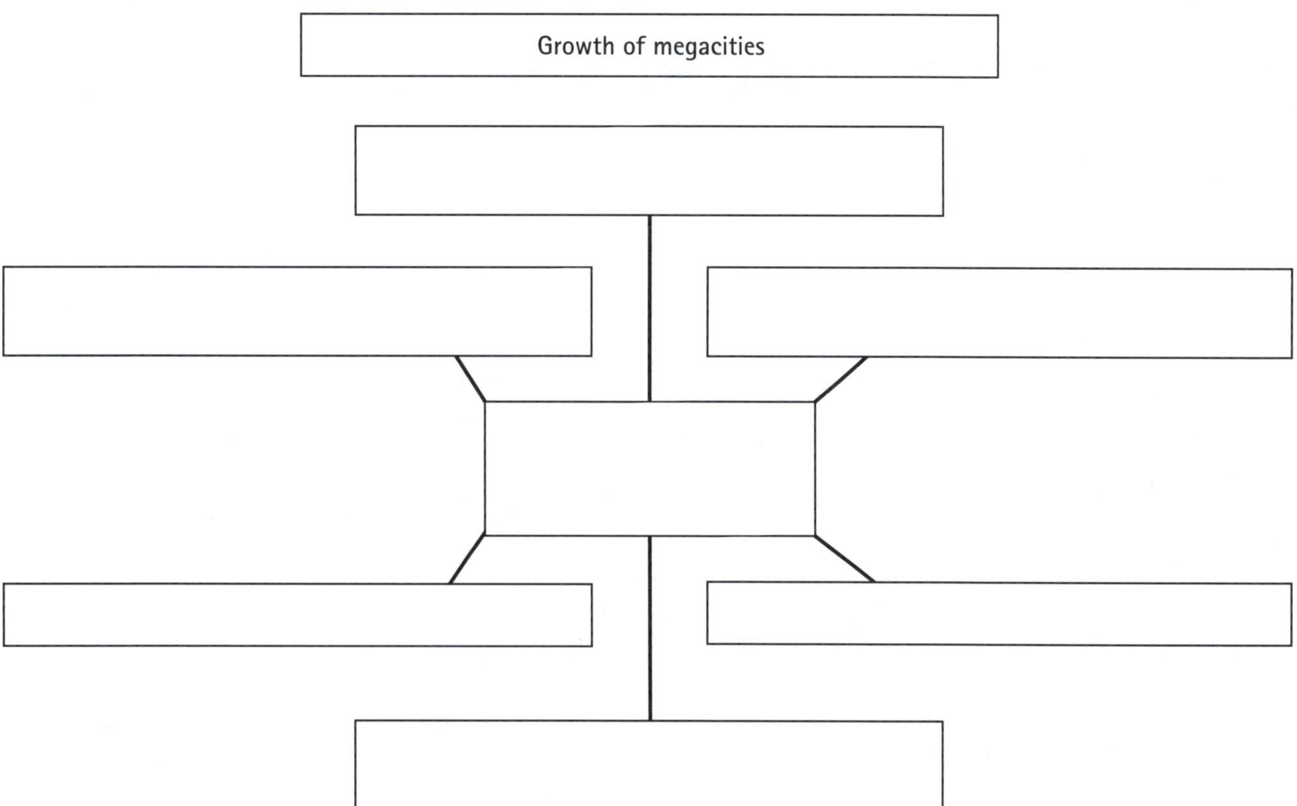

There are lots of ways you can create a mind map using a computer. Microsoft Word and Pages both have options in SmartArt to help you create a mind map and there are also apps for tablets and other smart devices that will help you construct a visual summary of what you have been studying.

Word clouds are also a good way to show the important factors in a concept. You can use a number of different apps available for Apple and Android devices to create word clouds and there are also websites such as Wordle™, Tagul and WordItOut. Above is a 'sustainability' word cloud.

ISBN 9780170367073

UNIT 28
VENN DIAGRAMS

A Venn diagram is made up of two or more overlapping circles and is a good way to compare two or more different sets of information. You will also use them in Mathematics to compare sets of numbers.

A Venn diagram will quickly show you the similarities and differences between the features or events that you are comparing.

The Venn diagram to the right has two features: A and B. Each has different characteristics (things that identify them) but there are some things that they have in common. The similarities between the two features are found in section C; the things that are unique about each feature are found in either section A or B.

A

Cyclone

- forms over water
- calm eye
- wide area of damage
- hours warning

C

Weather hazard
Rain
High wind
Damage to property
Loss of income
Possible injury or loss of life

B

Tornado

- forms over land
- violent eye
- focused path
- minutes warning

1 Fill in the Venn diagram below, using the following data.

Volcanic eruption

- Can kill people
- Caused by plate movement in the Earth's crust
- Magma pushed to the surface through a weakness in the Earth's crust
- Lava, ash and gases released
- Extreme natural event

Earthquake

- Extreme natural event
- Violent movements of Earth's crust
- Sends out shock waves
- Can kill people
- Caused by plate movement in the Earth's crust

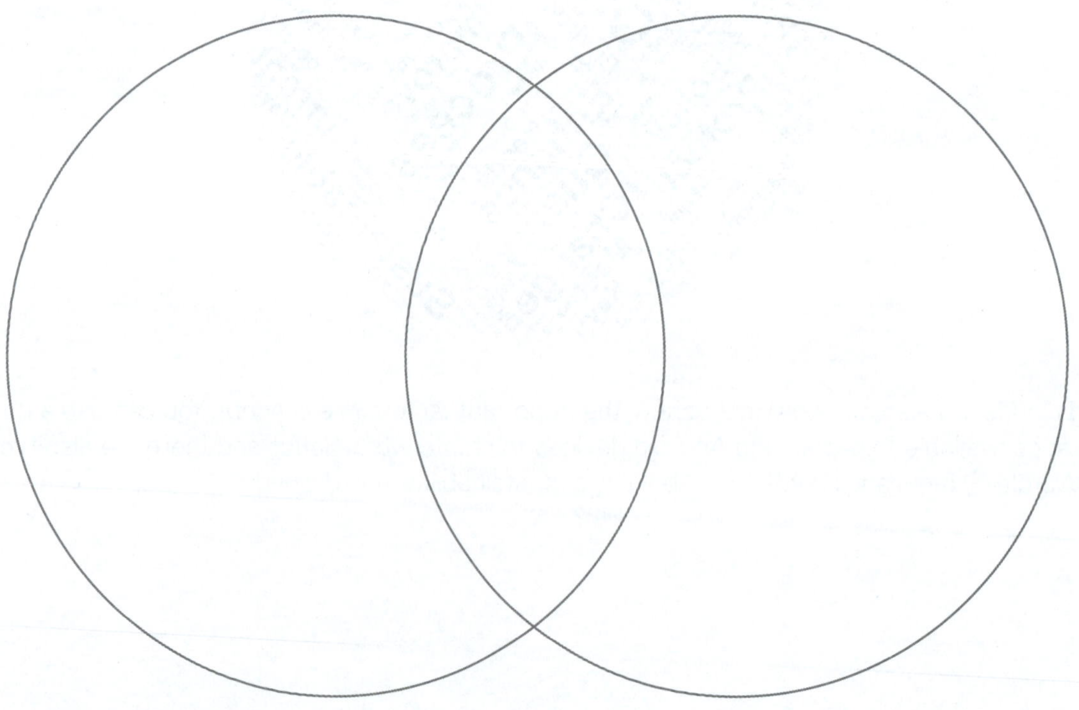

 ISBN 9780170367073

UNIT 29
SYSTEM DIAGRAMS

A **system** is a collection of parts that perform a job. A **system diagram** is a representation of how the system should work. A system may be something that operates in nature, something that humans have created or it may operate in social settings.

Whatever the type of system, there are four main parts of any system, as the diagram below shows.

Diagram of a beach system

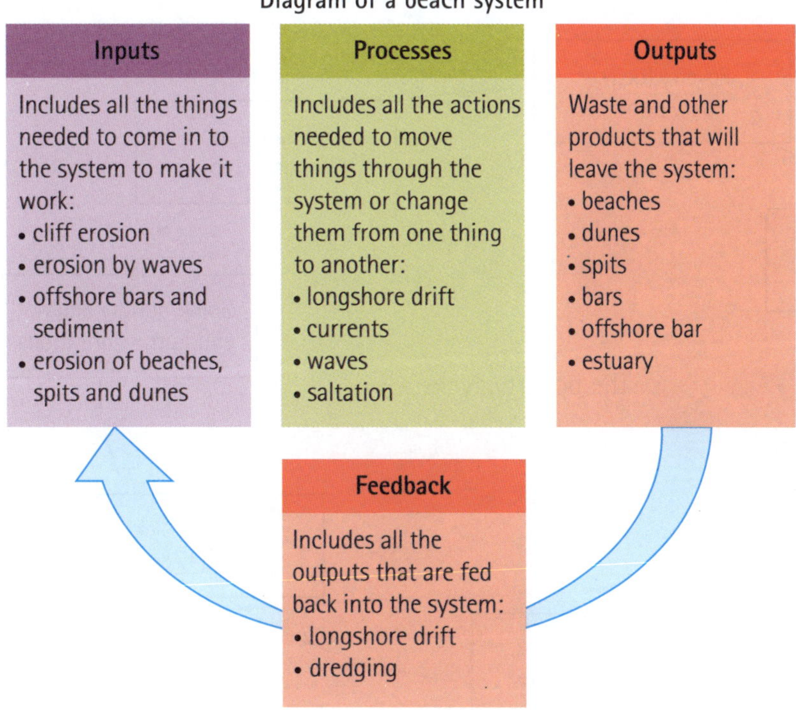

1 Write the following terms into the correct sections of the system diagram for a mature forest. Some have been completed for you.

evapotranspiration, photosynthesis, rainfall, solar energy, oxygen, seeds, bedrock, leaching, ground water, through flow, decay, water, plant decay

A forest system

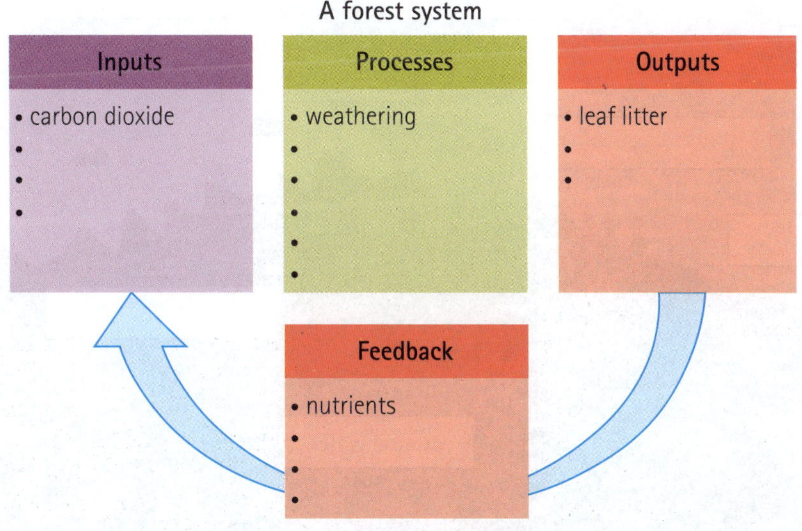

ISBN 9780170367073

UNIT 30
CYCLES

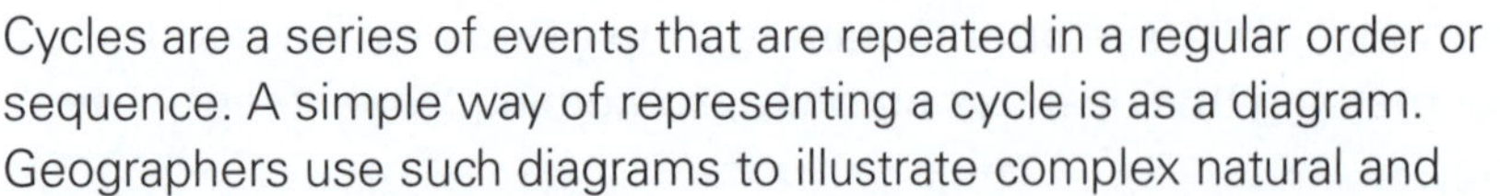

Cycles are a series of events that are repeated in a regular order or sequence. A simple way of representing a cycle is as a diagram. Geographers use such diagrams to illustrate complex natural and human cycles. A cycle diagram can show events of any length of time – day, week, month, year, years. In many Economically Less Developed Countries (ELDC), people are trapped in a poverty **cycle**. The diagram below illustrates the poverty cycle.

The word **cycle** comes from *kyklos* in Greek, meaning 'a circle'.

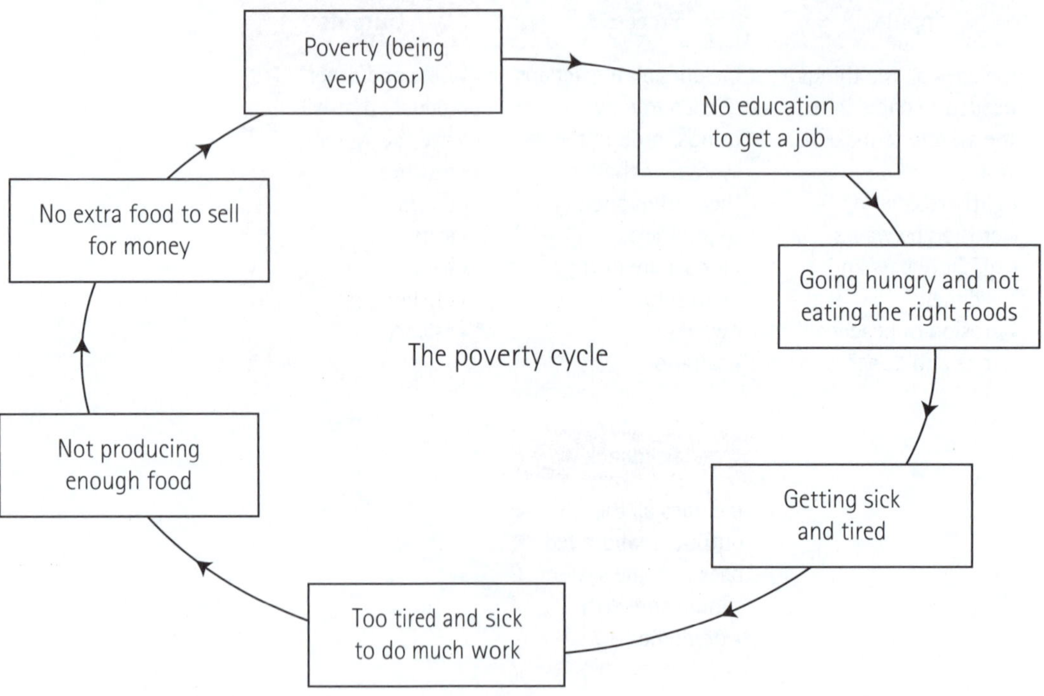

1 Not all cycles are presented in a simple circle diagram. The following diagram shows the water cycle. Complete it by placing the following words in the correct locations on the diagram.

condensation   run-off   transpiration   precipitation   percolation

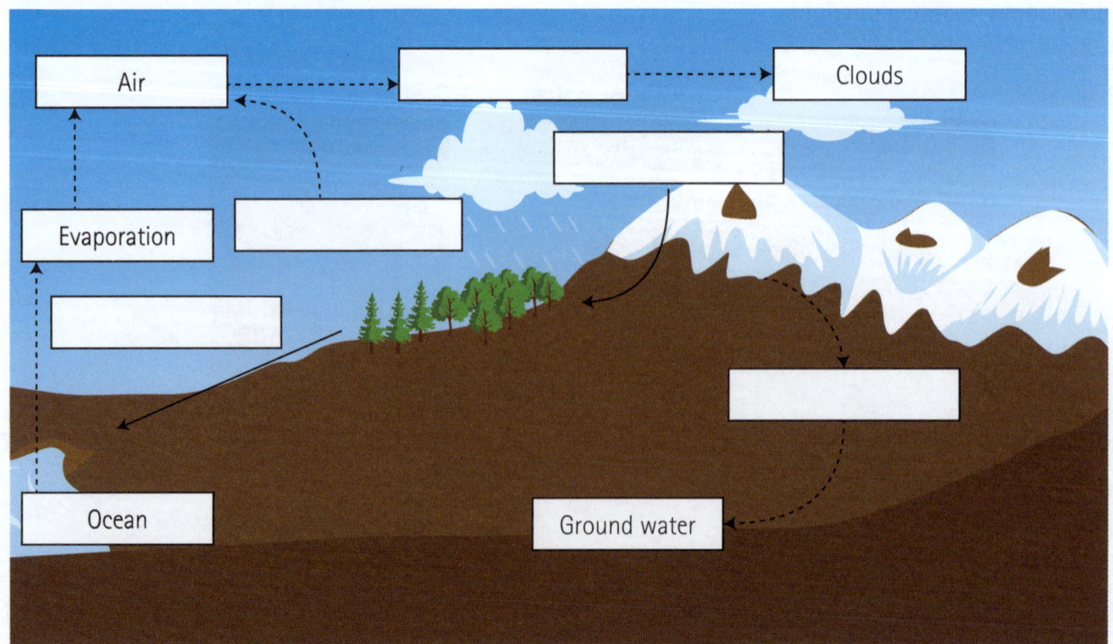

ISBN 9780170367073

2 Below is the cycle for the process of recycling paper:

- Collection – the bin is emptied and weighed by a specially designed truck and the paper is delivered to a nearby processing centre.
- Processing centre – the centre processes newspapers, magazines, office papers, school papers, shopping catalogues and mail. At the centre the mixed paper is sorted through to remove any contaminants such as plastic and cardboard.
- Cleaners and screens – paper is delivered to the mill and sent through a pulper. Warm water, soap and a series of screens help remove foreign materials. This creates a mix called a slurry.
- Washing – after moving over fine screens, the slurry is separated with water, removing the remaining ink and other contaminants.
- Forming – a big roller irons out the mixture and removes all the excess moisture, creating recycled paper.
- Marketplace – the rolls of paper are then packed and ready for shipment to local printers, offices, packaging manufacturers and other users.
- Community – the money that it receives for the paper enables the community processing centre to fund special projects throughout the year.

Complete the paper recycling cycle diagram to show the activities that take place during the recycling of paper. There are images included to help you place the correct description in each place.

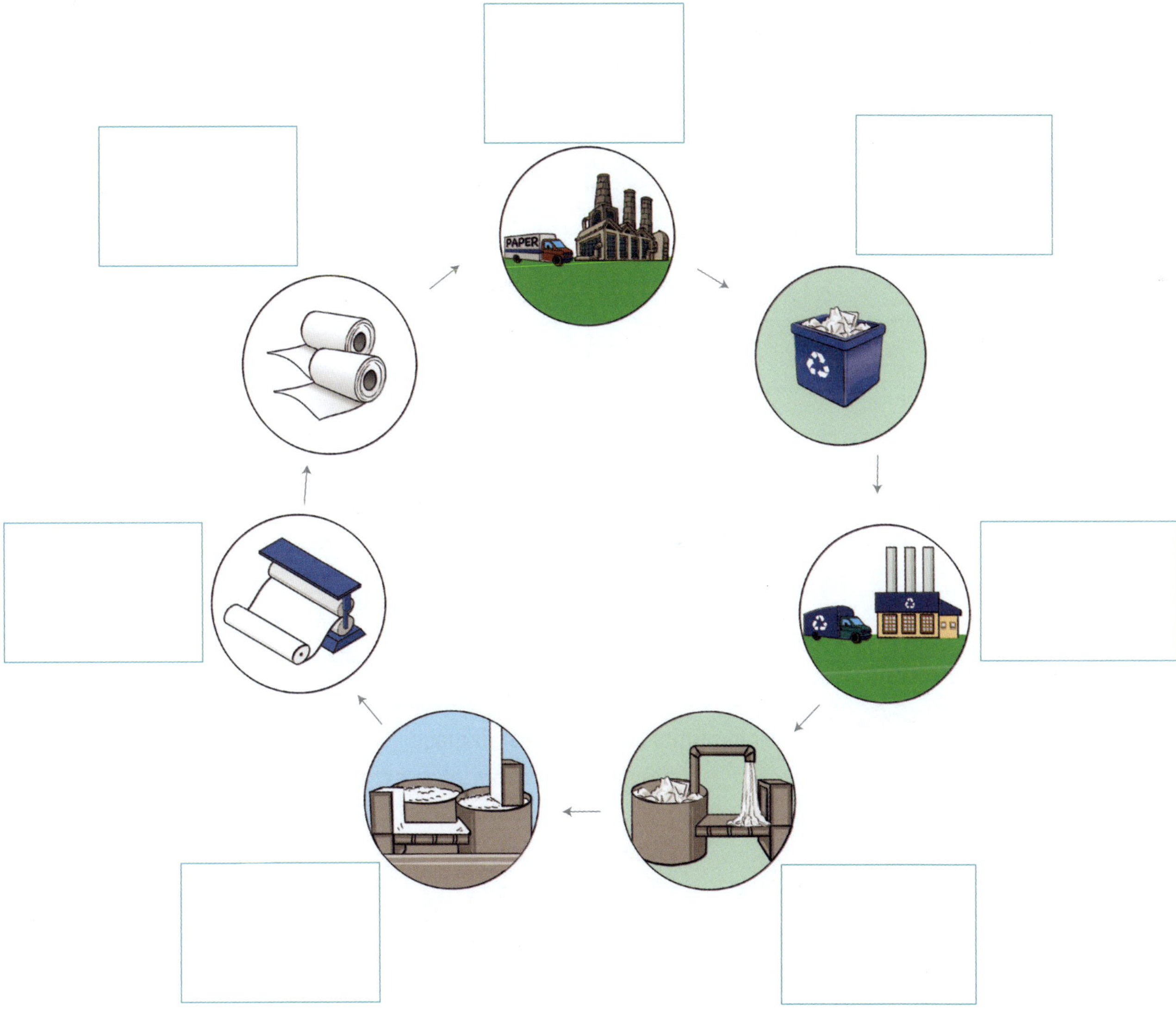

UNIT 31
FLOW CHARTS

A **flow chart** shows the order in which things take place. The title tells you what that thing is. The data on a flow chart flows in order, much like the way water in a river flows. Each part of a flow chart 'flows' into the next part, which then flows into the next part and so on. Arrows show the order of flow.

1 Write the following four pieces of data into the correct boxes of the flow chart below:
The Defence Force gives help straight away; Crops are replanted; Warnings are given out to people; The tropical cyclone arrives

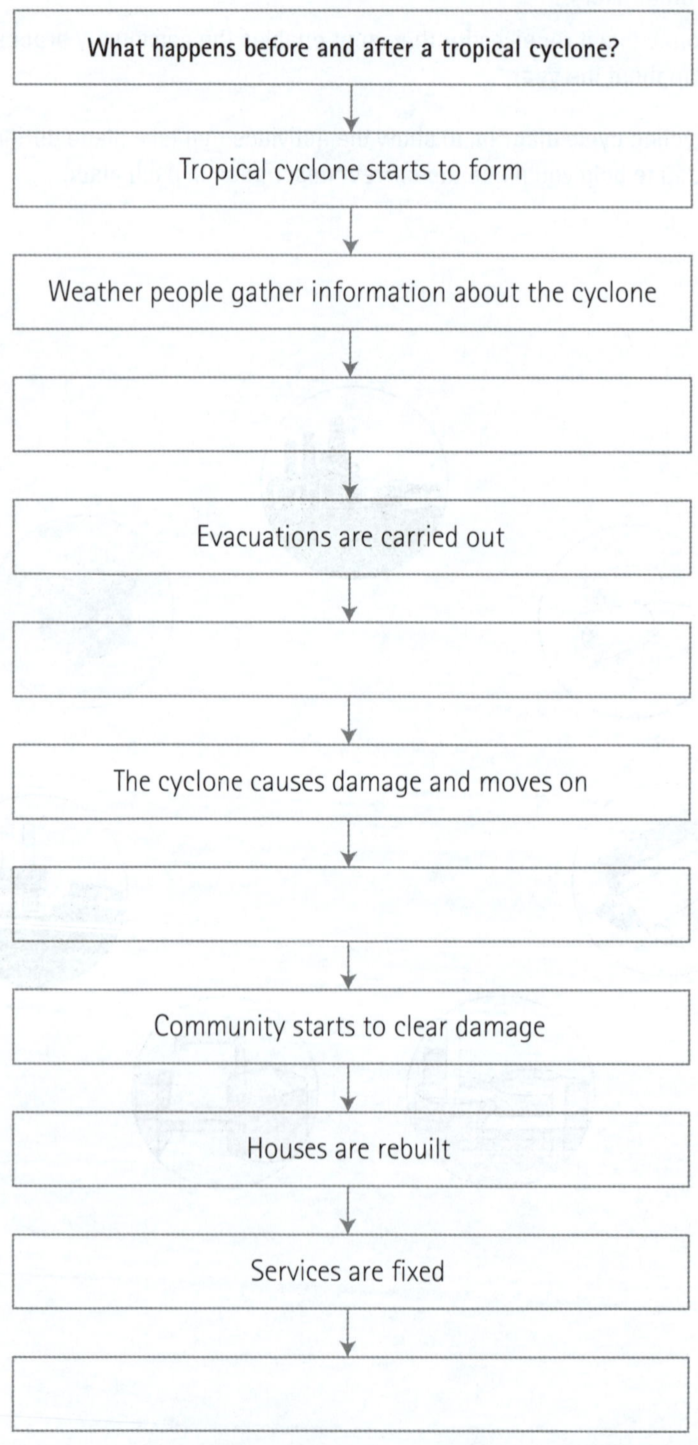

 ISBN 9780170367073

2 Write the following five pieces of data into the correct boxes of the flow chart below:

- All bark and branches are removed and left at the logging site
- Logs are watered by sprinklers to prevent cracking and splitting
- Logs are broken down by a bandsaw to maximise profit
- After being trimmed and graded, logs are loaded onto trucks and sent to the saw mill
- The best timber is left to dry for another 12 months and then kiln-dried for 7 days

The logging process at Toolangi

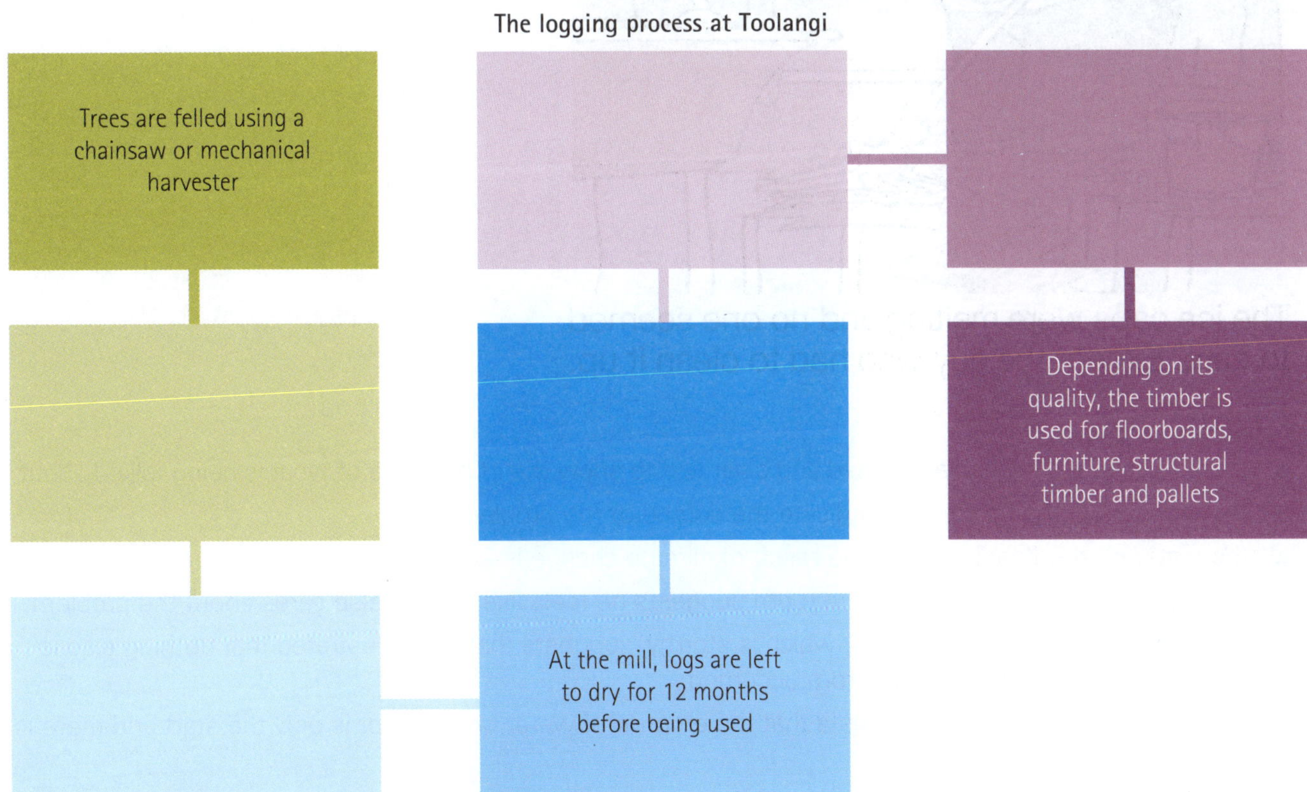

GROUP ACTIVITY

In groups of three or four, use a large piece of paper and different coloured pens to discuss the issue of logging in old growth forests.

E = Excited

What are the benefits of logging?

W = Worrisome

What are the geographical issues related to logging?

N = Need to know

What additional information would help you to evaluate the true costs and benefits of logging?

S = Stance or Suggestion for moving forward

What is your current opinion about logging? Is there a way that your opinion could be altered or modified?

UNIT 32
CARTOONS

Cartoons can be used to convey a complex message with a simple image. The cartoon below is an example of this.

A **cartoon** is a drawing that:

- is about a person, people or event
- has a message or something it wants you to think about
- gives the artist's opinion on a topic
- usually aims to be funny and make you smile
- may exaggerate or draw things in a larger-than-life way to grab your attention
- should be easy to understand and read.

www.CartoonStock.com/Mike Baldwin

The ice caps were melting and no one seemed to care. Except the guy who had to clean it up.

In this cartoon:

- there are some simple images used and clear text to show the importance of what is being talked about
- the factories in the background indicate the source of the problem
- the water on the floor indicates the result of climate change is evident now
- the fact that the man is alone in the room suggests he feels like no one else cares about the problem
- the thinking cloud above the man, which is stormy, suggests that he is frustrated that nothing else is being done to stop the problem from occurring
- the large head on the mop suggests that the amount of water on the floor is only the start and there is more to come.

In general, the cartoon suggests that climate change is a problem for which we know both the cause and the solution but we need to work together to solve the problem at the source and not just clean up the outcomes individually.

1 Imaging you are writing a Twitter post (a tweet) to describe the message from the cartoon 'Traffic Gridlock in the Future'. What would you say and what hashtags would you use (remember you only have 140 characters)?

____

____

____

Inkcinct Cartoons

ISBN 9780170367073

2 Examine the cartoon 'The El Ninny Effect' and answer the questions that follow.

Cartoon by Nicholson from *The Australian* www.nicholsoncartoons.com.au

a The name of the cartoonist (person who drew the cartoon) is ______________________.

b You can tell the cartoon is referring to Australia because of ______________________.

c There are three groups of people that appear in a drought. They are ______________, ______________ and ______________.

d The 'El Ninny Effect' refers to which effect that causes drought in Australia? E______ N______________.

e The three processes being talked about in the water cycle are ______________, ______________, and ______________.

f From the pictures, who do you think is the most likely group the government is giving money to? ______________

g Why is the money given to them? ______________________

h Circle six words in the box below that would be the best ones to use if you had to write about the meaning of this cartoon.

El Niño	farming	flood	pasture
water	pollution	drought	politics
fertilisers	water cycle	subsidies	ocean

ISBN 9780170367073

UNIT 33
INTERPRETING RESOURCES

There are four mains steps to the interpretation of resources:

- ▲ Study the **title**.
- ▲ Look at the source. A government agency such as the Department of Infrastructure and Regional Development has a reputation to safeguard so its facts are likely to be accurate.
- ▲ Read the **main idea in the introduction** to see what the story is about.
- ▲ Highlight the **main ideas in each paragraph** and in the conclusion.

Interpretation = making sense of
Resource = any material containing data and information, such as a map or graph or piece of writing

Resource 1

Government expands protection for the Coral Sea

Media Release from the Department of Infrastructure and Regional Development, 16 May 2015

The International Maritime Organization (IMO) has agreed to the Australian Government's proposed extension of the Great Barrier Reef and Torres Strait **Particularly Sensitive Sea Area (PSSA) to protect the South-West Coral Sea**.

Overnight the IMO Marine Environment Protection Committee in London agreed to the new arrangements, which will see an **additional 565 000 square kilometres of the South-West Coral Sea added to the existing** Great Barrier Reef and Torres Strait PSSA – a 140 per cent increase on the current 403 000 square kilometres.

Deputy Prime Minister and Minister for Infrastructure and Regional Development Warren Truss said the adoption of the new PSSA **will better protect this beautiful and unique oceanic region**. 'The Coral Sea is one of the world's most distinctive and undisturbed marine ecosystems,' Mr Truss said. 'It behoves us to do all we can to reasonably and responsibly protect one of our greatest natural resources. Our new measures enhance protection for the Coral Sea – as well as the adjacent Great Barrier Reef World Heritage area – by helping ships traverse the region safely and avoid potentially hazardous areas. This is a concrete example of the Australian Government taking the necessary steps to protect the Great Barrier Reef, implementing measures outlined in the North East Shipping Management Plan released in October 2014.'

Designation as a **PSSA helps to protect seas where significant ecological, socio-economic or scientific attributes may be vulnerable to damage by international shipping**. The Great Barrier Reef was declared the world's first PSSA in 1990. Three Associated Protective Measures will support the new PSSA, including a new Area to be Avoided and two supporting two-way routes. These measures will enhance ship safety by keeping traffic away from the many reefs, cays, islets, sandbars and shoal patches within the area. This reduces the risk of groundings and allows more time for intervention in developing situations, such as a ship suffering a mechanical breakdown.

The PSSA will come into effect once the Associated Protective Measures are adopted by the IMO Maritime Safety Committee, expected in June. **The APMs would come into effect six months later**. The Australian Maritime Safety Authority (AMSA) represents Australia at the IMO to develop standards for ship safety, prevention of marine pollution from ships, search and rescue and maritime communications.

'Government expands protection for the Coral Sea', Media Release from the Department of Infrastructure and Regional Development, May 2015

1 Read Resource 1 and circle the correct answers to the following statements.

a The total area under protection after the agreement is:

i 565 000 km^2 ii 403 000 km^2 iii 968 000 km^2.

b The Great Barrier Reef was declared a PSSA in:

i 2014 ii 1990 iii 2000.

c If approved, the protective measures will come into effect in:

i December ii June iii August.

ISBN 9780170367073

2 Read Resource 2 and complete the following.

a Use a highlighter to identify the title.

b Use a different colour to highlight the source and date.

c Circle the source of the data that the journalist used in the article.

d Underline the words in the first paragraph that describe the recovery work being done by the armies.

e Underline the words in the final paragraph that outline how Australia can help.

Resource 2

Australia-NZ 'teamwork vital' in rebuild

Military support was also provided by French, British and New Zealand defence forces, the ADF said. 'As with the Australian Defence Force operations in southern Vanuatu, the New Zealand troops have been repairing schools and medical facilities and have undertaken significant route clearance tasks,' it said. 'This teamwork has been vital to get remote communities back on their feet, with Black Hawk crew working in partnership with New Zealand Army engineers to deliver stores and aid from the New Zealand multi-role naval vessel HMNZS Canterbury.'

Aid agencies said while emergency relief flowed to those in need, many people in Vanuatu face longer-term problems. The UN's World Food Program said some of the worst affected cyclone victims might need ongoing help for several months.

The Australian Government said it would continue to support Vanuatu as it recovers from the cyclone. Foreign Minister Julie Bishop urged Australians to travel to Vanuatu once the initial crisis was over and use their tourist dollars to help rebuild the country. She said Australia would consider helping by expanding work opportunities for Vanuatu citizens as well as the $10 million of aid already pledged.

Cyclone Pam: Australian Defence Force completes recovery operation in Vanuatu, 17 April 2015.

3 Read Resource 3 and put a tick or cross in the boxes to show whether the statements beside them are true or false.

a The job is in a tropical location. ☐

b The job does not pay very much. ☐

c Only men are able to apply for the job. ☐

d You need to contact Ernest Shackleton if you are interested. ☐

e There is no doubt the trip will be a success. ☐

Resource 3

MEN WANTED

for hazardous journey, small wages, bitter cold, long months of complete darkness, constant danger, safe return doubtful, honour and recognition in case of success.

Ernest Shackleton
4 Burlington st.

UNIT 34
ISSUES AND OPINIONS

Australia has freedom of speech. This means people are allowed to have their own opinions about issues and say them out loud. You can't force other people to have the same opinions as you. This is not always the case in different parts of the world.

An **issue** = an event or a series of events on which people have a range of *opinions*.

The issue: Whaling

Whaling is an issue that has interested Australians for a long time. As early as the 1790s, Sydney Cove was the centre of a whaling trade that extended to the southern coast of Australia. In 1946 the International Whaling Commission (IWC) was set up to manage whaling. Australia was one of the first countries to sign an international agreement that aimed to conserve and manage whale stocks. In 1979 Australia decided to follow the IWC's ban on commercial whaling. Most other countries did the same. But today, the issue is that some IWC members continue to allow whaling; those countries claim they are doing it for scientific research.

Well, there's a cannon with a harpoon at the bow: We have to assume they're not here to study us...

Some opinions about whaling

Modern technology means whaling doesn't involve cruelty.

Scientific research is just an excuse to sell whale meat.

Whales don't hunt us, so why should we hunt them?

We need whales alive in the oceans so people can go whale watching.

Commercial whaling isn't necessary to supply any essential human need.

Different types of issues

Geographic issues can occur on a number of different scales:

Local	Regional	National	International	Global
e.g. should bike lanes be introduced in your community	e.g. recovery from a cyclone in far north Queensland	e.g. damage to the Australian coast through pollution	e.g. palm plantations replacing rainforest	e.g. climate change

Contemporary issue = going on right now (e.g. the logging of tropical rainforests)

Historical issue = has been around for a long time (e.g. a 50-year-old argument over logging in a native forest)

Geographic issue = related to people and places (e.g. Mr X logged five jarrah giants in a Western Australian native forest)

ISBN 9780170367073

Example of a contemporary, geographic and regional issue

Is Australia's Gold Coast a good place to live?

Some opinions:

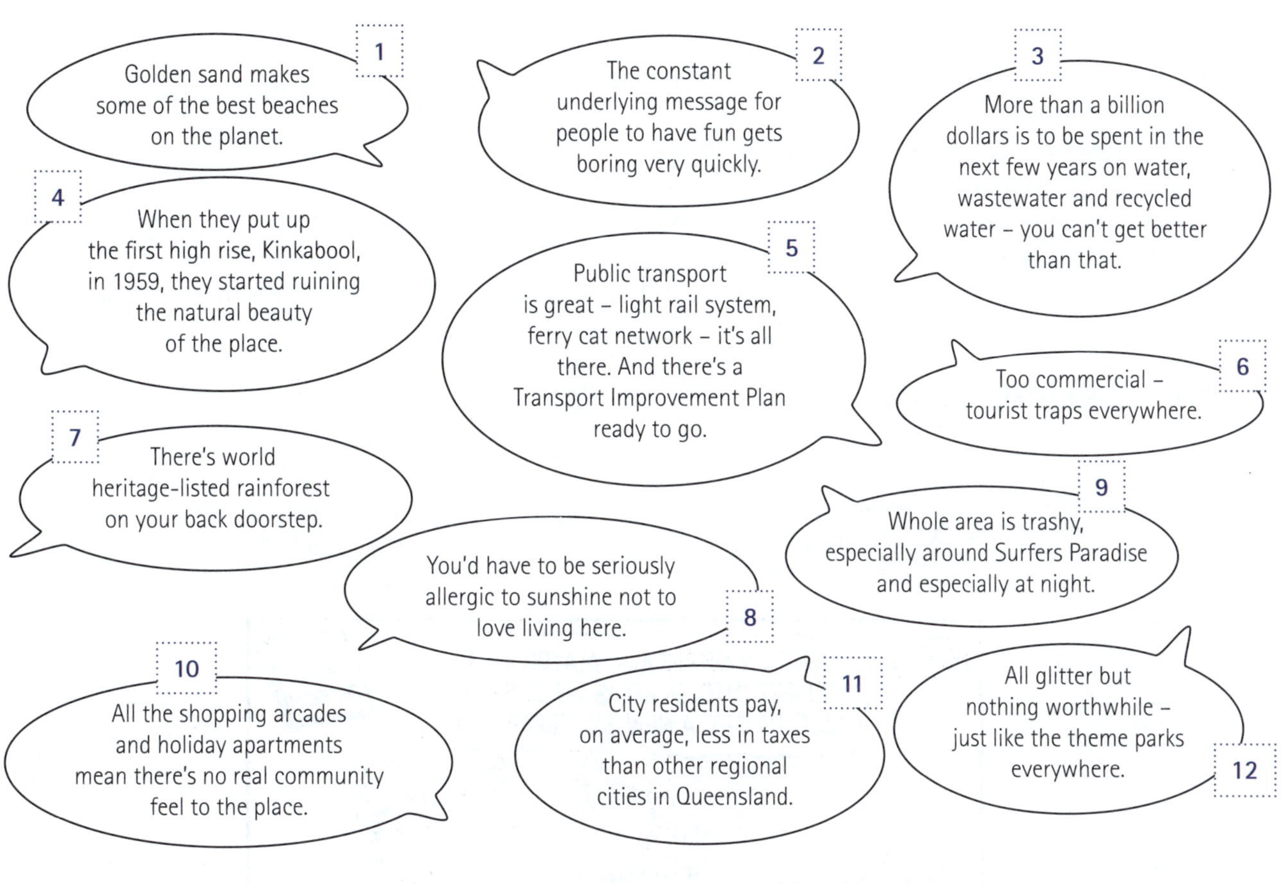

1 Review the opinions about the Gold Coast above. For each opinion, place a tick in the table below for a positive opinion (thinks the Gold Coast is a good place to live) and a cross for a negative opinion (does not think the Gold Coast is a good place to live).

Opinion:	1	2	3	4	5	6	7	8	9	10	11	12

2 Write down whether the following issues are mainly local, regional, national, international or global. (Answers may fit into more than one category.)

a Australia's asylum-seeker policies ______________________

b Bayside City Council's handling of housing developments ______________________

c Impact of global warming on world agricultural production ______________________

d Problems of growing population in sub-Saharan Africa ______________________

e Fixing earthquake damage in Nepal ______________________

ISBN 9780170367073

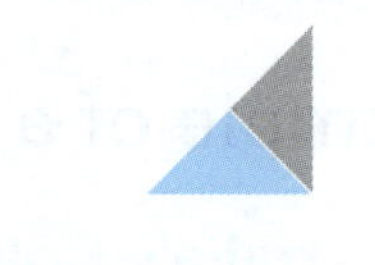

UNIT 35
VALUE CONTINUUMS

When people make a value judgement, they decide if something is good or bad according to their own values.

People's background, culture, age, sex, personality, education, religion, socioeconomic group and job can make a difference to what they value.

If a person is going to get something positive out of a proposed change, that person will probably encourage the change.

If a person is going to get something negative out of a proposed change, that person will probably discourage the change.

Values are standards on which people base their actions or opinions. They are things people consider to be important in life.

Proposed skateboard park

There are more important things in life.

Nothing's more important than skateboarding.

Don't need a park.

Need a park.

Would rather see a temple built there.

Skating's like a way of life. You need a place to follow your way of life.

Cartoon by Ron Seddon

Will be great for when my grandchildren come to stay.

It'll disturb my peace and quiet.

A **continuum** is a continuous line between two extremes to show how people feel about a particular issue. In between the three points, for, neutral and against, are lots of other positions.

100% FOR	NEUTRAL neither for nor against	100% AGAINST

ISBN 9780170367073

A Desalination Plant

Ellen Smith/Newspix

The proposal to build and operate a desalination plant to convert salt water to fresh water in the town of Wonthaggi, south-east Victoria, generated much public debate. The various groups involved had different positions on a continuum, such as:

- **Local community**: Employed thousands of workers during the building process and 52 workers keep the plant going while bringing increased spending in the local community
- **State and federal governments**: Needed a hard-handed approach to ensure Victoria's water future into the era of extended El Niño and climate change.
- **The Greens**: Fought against the construction of the desalination plant because of the energy needed to convert the water and the damage that can potentially be done to the marine environment
- **Aquasure**: Won the contract to build and operate the desalination plant and has a guaranteed income until 2039 for water supply
- **Watershed Victoria**: Argued that a sustainable water solution should have been found, rather than having taxpayers paying for water at an inflated price for 30 years
- **Local contractors**: More than $1 million in contracts were awarded to local companies in the construction of the plant and the infrastructure needed to support it

1 In each box on the continuum below, write the name of the group that is most likely to hold that position about the Wonthaggi plant.

To develop and operate a desalination plant in Wonthaggi, Victoria

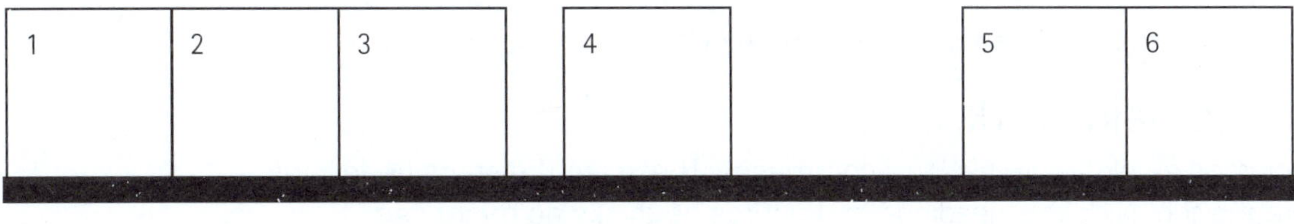

FOR AGAINST

It is interesting that, although the desalination plant was completed in 2012, it is now in standby mode as the government has not ordered any water from it because the need for water has decreased.

UNIT 36
FIELD WORK

Field work shows you a view of the natural and cultural environments and how they interact.

Field = a place where a particular activity takes place or the location of a particular environment

Field work = observation = seeing, watching, looking at, taking note of, putting theory into practice

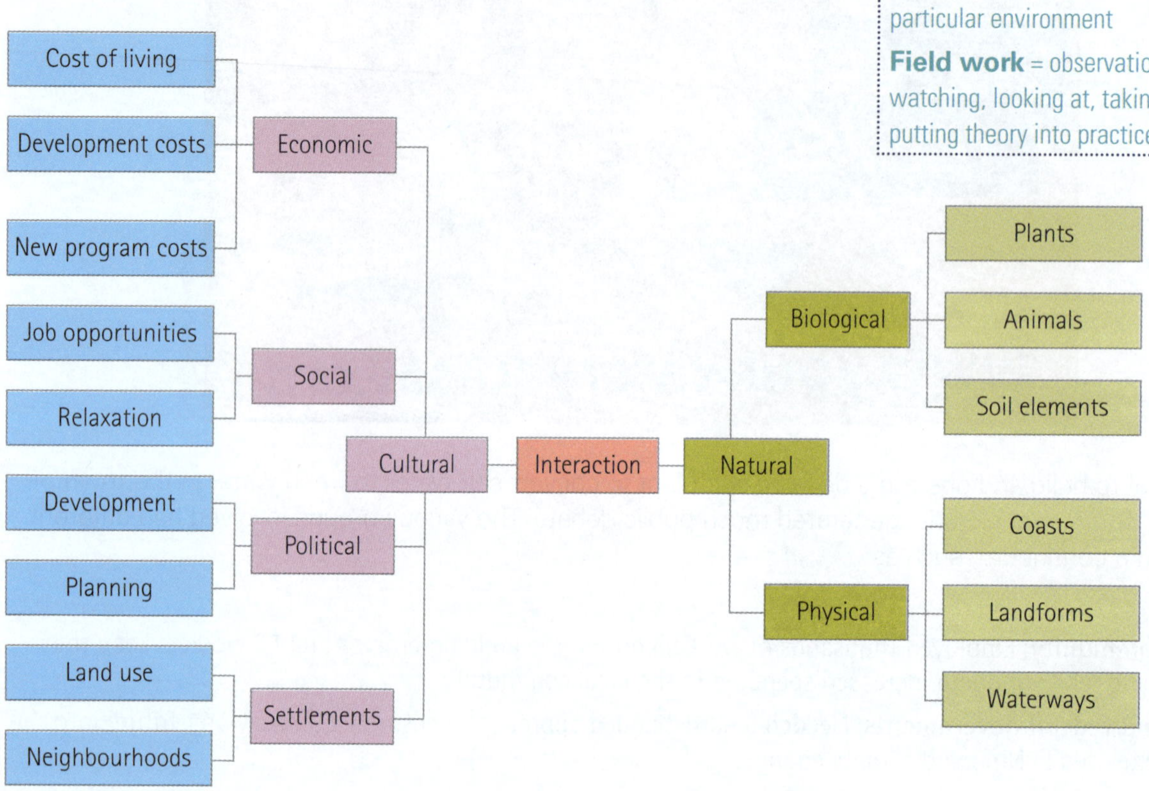

- Interaction
  - Cultural
    - Economic
      - Cost of living
      - Development costs
      - New program costs
    - Social
      - Job opportunities
      - Relaxation
    - Political
      - Development
      - Planning
    - Settlements
      - Land use
      - Neighbourhoods
  - Natural
    - Biological
      - Plants
      - Animals
      - Soil elements
    - Physical
      - Coasts
      - Landforms
      - Waterways

Why should you develop observation skills?

Developing observational skills:

- is helpful in emergencies; for example, noticing when something does not look as it should in the space around you
- allows you to apply the ideas and thoughts that you have about environments to the theories you have studied in class
- develops your problem solving and creative thinking skills
- allows you to explore spaces that you may not otherwise visit and gives you a chance to be out of a classroom
- teaches you to classify features into natural and cultural categories
- allows you to see interactions first hand
- gives you the chance to reflect on your interactions with these places.

How to do field work

Nick is going on a field trip to his local community. These are the steps he follows.

1. Before the trip, Nick lists headings for features he thinks he might see.
2. At the main street of his community, Nick makes notes beside the headings on his list.
3. Nick adds other features he sees that are not on his list.
4. After the trip, Nick tidies his notes and makes some general comments about what he saw.

ISBN 9780170367073

Nick's headings

Buildings (B)
Natural features (NF)
Transport (Tr)
People (P)
Tourist features (TF)
Management (M)
Developments (D)

Nick's notes of what he saw

shops for lease	B	new apartment building	
train station		traffic lights	
banks		school	
chemist		streets	
footpath		speed humps	
car parks on street		seating	
trees on the nature strip		park	
playground		restaurants	
parking areas		supermarkets	
pedestrians		post office	
lots of parked cars		petrol station	
40-km zone		lake	
pedestrian lights			

1 In the boxes on Nick's notes, write the first letters of the headings that each note should go under. The first one has been done for you.

ISBN 9780170367073

UNIT 37
FIELD SKETCHING

What is a field sketch?

A **field sketch** is a freehand drawing. A photograph shows all features, but a field sketch shows only some features

When creating a field sketch:

- you don't have to be a great artist – you aren't judged on how well you draw
- your sketch should show how well you understand how features fit together
- you can sketch a scene or just one feature of it.

Field sketches are useful because they:

- show how features interact
- make you think about what you see
- encourage you to look more closely
- reduce a complicated subject to simple lines
- let you decide which features to draw and which ones to leave out
- let you explain what you see
- provide a summary of what you saw at a particular time and place.

Important things to include in sketches

Field sketches should include:

- title
- frame
- simple notes to explain features
- simple lines.

Sketch the horizon first, then the scene's big features. Try holding a pencil at arm's length to help you work out sizes of features. Make sure that your sketch is big enough so it isn't cluttered and hard to read.

Coastline of Rosebud Beach, 6 March 2014

ISBN 9780170367073

1 Use the photograph of the Yarra River in Melbourne to create a field sketch in the box below showing the Yarra River Precinct, Melbourne. Label each of the following features on your field sketch.

City skyline

Train station

Bridge

Cruise boat

Grass area

Dock

River

UNIT 38
SURVEYS

A **survey** (say **ser**-vay) is a way of collecting data about something that can be counted. It could be the amount of traffic, the number of pedestrians or the different types of shops on a street.

The sheet on which data is recorded is organised into headings and points before the survey is taken. Anyone or anything involved in the survey is given the same questions and survey sheets.

The surveyors take the survey sheets out to the survey location and collect the data there.

TRAFFIC SURVEY SHEET	
DATE: TIME: ROAD:	
Mode of transport	**Number**
bicycle	
car	
bus	
heavy truck	
light truck	
mobility scooter	
motorbike	
pedestrian	
skateboard	
taxi	
van	
Survey summary:	

Traffic survey

Traffic surveys are an important part of population studies.

They can be used to work out if the roads are adequate for the number of cars on the road or if there needs to be another transport alternative introduced in the area to take the pressure off a location.

To carry out a traffic survey you would go in a group to the main intersection in the area you are studying and each take a different corner of the intersection. For the next five minutes, each person in the group would count the traffic travelling in their allocated direction.

If a comparison of different areas was needed, you would move to different locations and repeat the same process as before.

After collecting the information in the survey, you can use a bar chart (see Unit 5) to present the data and compare the different areas or traffic and come to a conclusion about the road and transport needs in the area.

This same process is used by local councils on a larger scale in planning and development decision/s.

ISBN 9780170367073

1 Carry out a traffic survey at a location near you for five minutes and record your data on the survey sheet. When you return to school, collate (put it all together) the group's information and draw a bar chart of your results in the box below. Also write a one-paragraph summary of your survey.

2 Imagine there has been a storm that has caused damage in your neighbourhood. Fill out the following survey by ticking the boxes that apply for each category. Then write a summary of your survey.

SURVEY AIM: TO FIND OUT ABOUT STORM DAMAGE

DATE:
TIME:
PLACE:

CATEGORY	A lot of damage	1	2	3	4	5	No damage
electricity	no power						no interruptions
telephone	cut off						no interruptions
trees	many down						none down
flooding	heavy flooding						no flooding
houses	a lot of damage						no damage
evacuations	many evacuated						no evacuations
animals	deaths/injuries						no deaths/injuries
people	deaths/injuries						no deaths/injuries
roads	heavy damage						no damage
schools	closed						no closures

Survey summary:

ISBN 9780170367073

UNIT 39 QUESTIONNAIRES

Questionnaire (say kwes-ch'n-air) is a French word that has come into the English language. It is a set of questions (on a printed form or online) to get a person's opinion or gather information for a survey.

You can send a questionnaire to people for them to fill out and send back to you. Or you can ask people the questions face-to-face and write their answers down.

The questions are the same for everyone you ask. This is different from an interview where you are trying to bring out a person's memories or opinions.

You need to decide how you will choose who will answer the questionnaire. It is important that you have enough answers to find out if there are any patterns and enough different people so you don't have a limited point of view.

There are many different ways that you can create a questionnaire on a computer and collate the answers automatically. Google Forms and SurveyMonkey® are both methods that can be used.

To make the questionnaire as simple as possible:

Tell people why you're doing the questionnaire and how long it will take.

First ask all the questions about what groups people fall into, so it's easier to sort questionnaires later.

Don't ask personal questions – instead give a range of choices for people to select from.

Use YES/NO answers or tick boxes.

Give an 'escape' in case people do not fit any of the choices offered.

Keep all the questions simple and short – don't use technical terms or words people may not understand, ask only what's important to your study, don't ask questions that suggest the answers.

Thank the people who complete the questionnaire for you.

Questionnaire

Reason for questionnaire: *I'm doing this for a school project to find out about the population of the town. It should take approximately 5 minutes.*

1 What is your gender? ☐ Female ☐ Male

2 What is your age? ☐ 0–15 ☐ 16–30 ☐ 31–45 ☐ 46–60 ☐ 61–75 ☐ 75+

3 In which country were you born?

☐ New Zealand	☐ Australia	☐ England
☐ Scotland	☐ Ireland	☐ Netherlands
☐ Vietnam	☐ Cambodia	☐ Fiji
☐ Italy	☐ Greece	☐ China
☐ Japan	☐ North Korea	☐ South Korea
☐ Other		

4 What is your current postcode? ☐

5 How long have you lived at your current address?

☐ less than 1 year ☐ 1–5 years ☐ 6–10 years ☐ more than 10 years

6 How many people live with you?

☐ none ☐ 1 ☐ 2 ☐ 3 ☐ 4 ☐ 5 ☐ more than 5

7 How many other places in Australia have you lived for more than 6 months? ☐

8 Have you lived in another country for a period of more than 6 months? Y/N

Thank you for taking the time to complete this questionnaire

ISBN 9780170367073

Questionnaire

Reason for questionnaire: *Local council wants to decide what recreational activities to include for young people in its five-year plan.*

1 What is your age? ☐ 5–8 ☐ 9–12 ☐ 13–16 ☐ 17–20 ☐ 21+

2 What are your five favourite recreational activities?

________________ ________________ ________________

________________ ________________

3 How often do you do these activities? ________________________________

4 When do you mostly do these activities?

☐ Before school ☐ After school ☐ Weekends ☐ Holidays ☐ Other

5 How do you get to the locations for these activities? __________________________

6 What is the approximate cost of getting to and into the places (include transport and entry costs)?

☐ Free ☐ <$5 ☐ $6–10 ☐ $11–20 ☐ >$20

7 How crowded are the facilities that you use regularly? Indicate on the scale below.

4 Overcrowded — 3 — 2 — 1 Not crowded at all

8 Which of your favourite activities need adult supervision?

____

9 Which of your favourite activities are not available in your area?

____

Thank you for taking the time to complete this questionnaire.

1. Fill out the questionnaires in this unit. Time how long each takes to complete.
2. Collect the information about favourite recreational activities from everyone in your class and create a bar graph in the box below to decide which activities should be supplied by your local council.

UNIT 40
FACTS AND OPINIONS

Facts and opinions in a discussion on the importance of rainforests

Fact = a statement that is true and can be backed up with proof

Example**:** One per cent of agricultural credit goes to African women.

Opinion = a statement that shows what a person believes although it may not be true or provable

Example**:** African women are more likely to be in low-paid jobs with poor conditions.

Facts about rainforests

- Forests cover 30 per cent of the Earth's land.
- The Amazon rainforest is the largest tropical rainforest in the world.
- The average temperature of the tropical rainforest remains between 20 °C and 34 °C.
- Twenty per cent of our oxygen is produced in the Amazon rainforest.
- Rainforests help to regulate the temperatures and weather patterns around the world.
- Just over half a hectare of forest is cut down every second.
- Tropical rainforests cover 6–7 per cent of the Earth's surface and contain more than half of all the plant and animal species in the world.

Things that are accepted as true and provable

Opinions about rainforests

- Insects make up the majority of living creatures in the tropical rainforest.
- Poverty, over-population and unequal land access are the main causes of man-made deforestation.
- You can find rainforests in Alaska and Canada, as well as Asia, Africa and Latin America.
- About a fifth of our fresh water is found in tropical rainforests.
- A variety of animals, including snakes, frogs, birds, insects, cougars, chameleons, turtles, jaguars and many more, are found in tropical rainforests.
- Approximately 57 per cent of rainforests are located in developing countries.
- About 90 per cent of people living in poverty worldwide depend on rainforests for their daily needs.

Things that not everyone accepts as true because there is not yet 100 per cent proof

ISBN 9780170367073

1 Write F (for fact) or O (for opinion) in the boxes beside the following statements about how to make a city sustainable. Clues for which statements are opinions are words such as 'think', 'should', 'could' and 'may', and statements about the future.

- a Clean, efficient and equitable cities can drive global transformation. ☐
- b Between the years 2000 and 2030, the entire built-up urban area in developing countries is projected to triple. ☐
- c Darwin may be the most sustainable city in Australia. ☐
- d Two-thirds of the world's population live in cities. ☐
- e Sustainable cities would provide efficient, affordable and healthy transport choices. ☐
- f If a population of a city doubles, then its built area triples. ☐
- g More than 80 per cent of global GDP is generated in cities. ☐
- h Current global municipal solid waste production per year is 1.3 billion tonnes. ☐

2 Write F (for fact) or O (for opinion) in the boxes beside the following statements about world population.

- a A country's 'ecological footprint' is the land or sea needed to produce what a country consumes and where waste is disposed. ☐
- b The world's population will ruin all its natural resources. ☐
- c Each person on the planet has an average ecological footprint of 1.7 hectares. ☐
- d Australia's average ecological footprint is 6.25 hectares. ☐
- e The human population is growing too quickly. ☐
- f Humans should colonise at least one more 'earth' by the year 2050. ☐
- g The US average ecological footprint is 8.0 hectares. ☐
- h The average ecological footprint for an African or Asian person is less than 1.4 hectares. ☐
- i Australians are living way beyond what is sustainable. ☐

Research has been improved in the area of monitoring of seismic waves and the technology that is being used now means it is likely that up to 30 seconds warning can be given to people. 'This would mean that governments could have enough time to shut down essential services before they are damaged,' said a disaster management expert.

3 a Underline in red the 18 words that make the key fact in the above paragraph.

b Underline in blue an opinion in the above paragraph.

GROUP ACTIVITY

In pairs, think about an issue of sustainability in your local area.

1 Write a headline that captures the most important aspects of the local sustainability issue.

2 Write a small article for the local newspaper that goes with your headline and include four facts and three opinions.

3 Then write down the things that you discussed today that you would not have thought about yesterday if you had not considered the difference between facts and opinions.

UNIT 41
WRITING PARAGRAPHS

A Mathematics formula will help you work out a tricky Mathematics problem. A writing formula will help you work out a tricky writing problem – that is, how to organise your ideas on paper so they make sense to someone reading them.

A popular writing formula is GEED. Each letter in the GEED formula stands for something (see the definition box on the right).

For example:

GEED

- ▲ **G**eneralisation (a general statement of what the topic is about)
- ▲ **E**xplanation (expanding the generalisation by giving more information)
- ▲ **E**xample (something that illustrates the generalisation or shows that it is true)
- ▲ **D**iagram (a sketch or image about something to do with the topic)

G

Landcare is a national network of more than 5000 community groups and many thousands of volunteers in most towns across Australia. There are more than 11 000 schools and youth groups registered on the National Landcare Directory, which is managed by Landcare Australia. It proves that citizenship can do great things for the environment.

E

Around 73 per cent of farmers feel that they are part of the Landcare movement and many more practise Landcare farming. There are Rivercare groups, Coastcare groups and Urban Landcare groups to look after river, coastal, and town and city environments.

E

Each year landcarers plant many millions of native trees, shrubs and grasses for a range of benefits, such as better soils, water and air quality, and protection for thousands of native species.

D

The image at left is the Landcare logo. It is in the shape of two hands holding Australia. Tasmania is cleverly put in as part of a hand. The logo shows a caring attitude to Australia. It shows how willing hands are helping to repair and protect the land. This is a good example of citizenship.

1 Sort the following parts of a paragraph into the order they should appear. Write each part in the space provided.

Parts:

a Example

b Diagram

c Generalisation

d Explanation

Order:

a ____________________

b ____________________

c ____________________

d ____________________

ISBN 9780170367073

2 Read the generalisation below and circle the letter beside the best explanation and example.

Generalisation = In Australia, different types of livestock farming are mainly concentrated in areas that best suit them.

a The best explanation to use with the generalisation would be:

i Water availability and climate conditions are important for deciding where livestock farming takes place.

ii Crops such as corn and apples are grown in the maritime climate zones along the south-eastern coast and in Tasmania.

b The best example to use with the generalisation would be:

i Sugar cane is a major crop in Queensland and New South Wales, where it is drier.

ii Most dairy cattle farming is found in the wetter southern states, especially in Victoria.

3 The table below has information that could help you write a good paragraph about sustainable development and Torres Strait Islanders. Choose which of the four pieces you would use. Write G, E, E and D into the small boxes to show your choices in writing a paragraph.

The Torres Strait Islander flag has a white Dari (headdress), which is a symbol of the Torres Strait Islander people.	**a**
The mother dugong holds her calf to her breast when rising to the surface and this may be where stories of mermaids come from.	**b**
Although thousands now live outside the area, Torres Strait Islanders come from the tropical islands between Cape York and New Guinea from where they travelled long distances in search of turtles and dugongs.	**c**
Traditionally they are a seafaring people. Dugongs and turtles are part of their culture, but today the Islanders want to share responsibility for the management of fisheries in the region.	**d**
Using sea resources wisely so they will be there for the future generations is important to Torres Strait Islanders.	**e**
Torres Strait Islands	**f**
In some parts of the world people live without ever seeing or using the sea.	**g**

UNIT 42
INTERNET RESEARCH

The Internet is a collection of a lot of different networks of computers all talking to each other, using the same rules of communication or protocols.

The Internet was introduced in the 1990s as an easily usable access format for information in the form of the World Wide Web (www), and meant that you could carry the information from an entire library around on your laptop – as long as you had Internet access!

Now anyone can access reliable, up-to-the-minute information to help with school assignments and work. But how do you know what information is worthwhile and where to find it?

"An encyclopedia? I don't know. Let's look up what it is on Wikipedia."

www.CartoonStock.com/Marty Bucella

Hint 1: When you find information you think is correct, check it in three more locations. Textbooks and libraries are still a great source of information.

Hint 2: Know what you are searching for. Google is a great resource, but it cannot read your mind. To get a specific answer, you need to ask a specific question:

- use quotation marks to narrow your search e.g. 'monsoon asia'
- use alternate spellings (e.g. colour or color)
- a minus sign before a key word means that it is to be omitted from the search results –
- do not insert spaces between the minus sign and the words that follow it.

Hint 3: Wikipedia is not a reliable source of information. Anyone can be an author on Wikipedia and they don't necessarily have to know much about the topic they have written about.

Hint 4: .edu sites *teach*
.com sites *sell*
.org sites *have an opinion*
.au sites are *in Australia*
.co sites are *not in Australia* (e.g. United Kingdom)

Hint 5: Check when the information was last updated – just because you can find information on the Internet doesn't mean it is recent.

Hint 6: Be selective, be brutal, be wise. If it seems too good to be true, it probably is. You can waste hours looking for information and find nothing. If you are losing time, walk away, check your textbook and start again.

ISBN 9780170367073

1 Answer the following questions about the web address http://www.google.com.

a www stands for ______________________________

b google is the name of a ______________________________

c com stands for ______________________________

2 Write three key words for an Internet search on the following topics.

a The population of Japan is ageing so quickly that it has big problems in providing for its increasing percentage of elderly folk.

____

b When the Indian Government promoted the issue of family planning in India, lots of people didn't like it and voted against the government.

____

3 Evaluate one of the following sources of information using the CARS method (see below).

- ▲ http://ngkids.com.au/
- ▲ http://kidzsearch.com/wiki/Geography
- ▲ http://allaboutexplorers.com/
- ▲ http://www.aljazeera.com/

CARS method

Credibility	Goal: A source that is created by a person or organisation who knows the subject and who cares about its quality
Is there a publishing or sponsoring organisation? Is the organisation an authority on the subject? Is the author listed? Is the author an authority on the subject? How do you know? Are there spelling errors, grammatical errors, dead links, or other problems that indicate a lack of quality control?	
Accuracy	**Goal: A source with information that is current, complete and correct**
Does the information on the website agree with other sources? Does the site contradict itself? What is the date of publication or copyright? How recently has the website been updated?	
Reasonableness	**Goal: A source that is truthful and unbiased**
Does the author, host, publisher or sponsor have a bias? What is the motivation or purpose for creating the website? (To sell a product? To advance a viewpoint or belief? To educate?)	
Support	**Goal: A source with verifiable sources of information**
Are the sources listed? Can they be checked? Is there a way to contact the author or organisation?	

Apps – If you have an iPad or android device, there are some apps you can use to help you find information via video and text:

- ▲ Khan Academy – teaching lessons, mainly on Mathematics and Science
- ▲ TED Talks – short (approximately 15-minute) videos covering a range of different topics
- ▲ Flipboard – searches the web and puts the information together for you, like a magazine

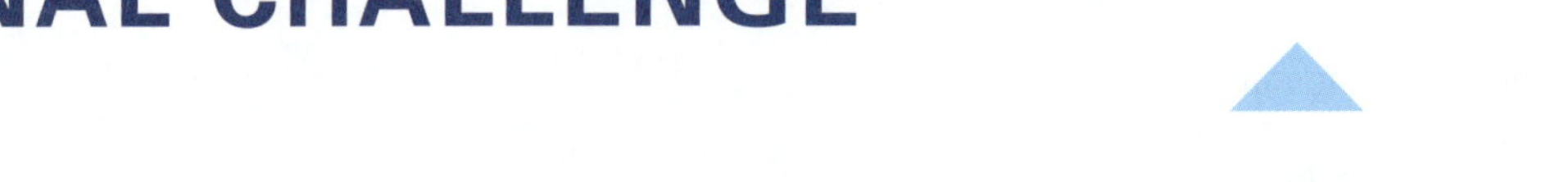

UNIT 43
FINAL CHALLENGE

The final challenge draws together all the Geography skills and concepts you have encountered in this book. Can you meet the challenge?

1 Name each of the geographic concepts represented by the acronym SPICESS.

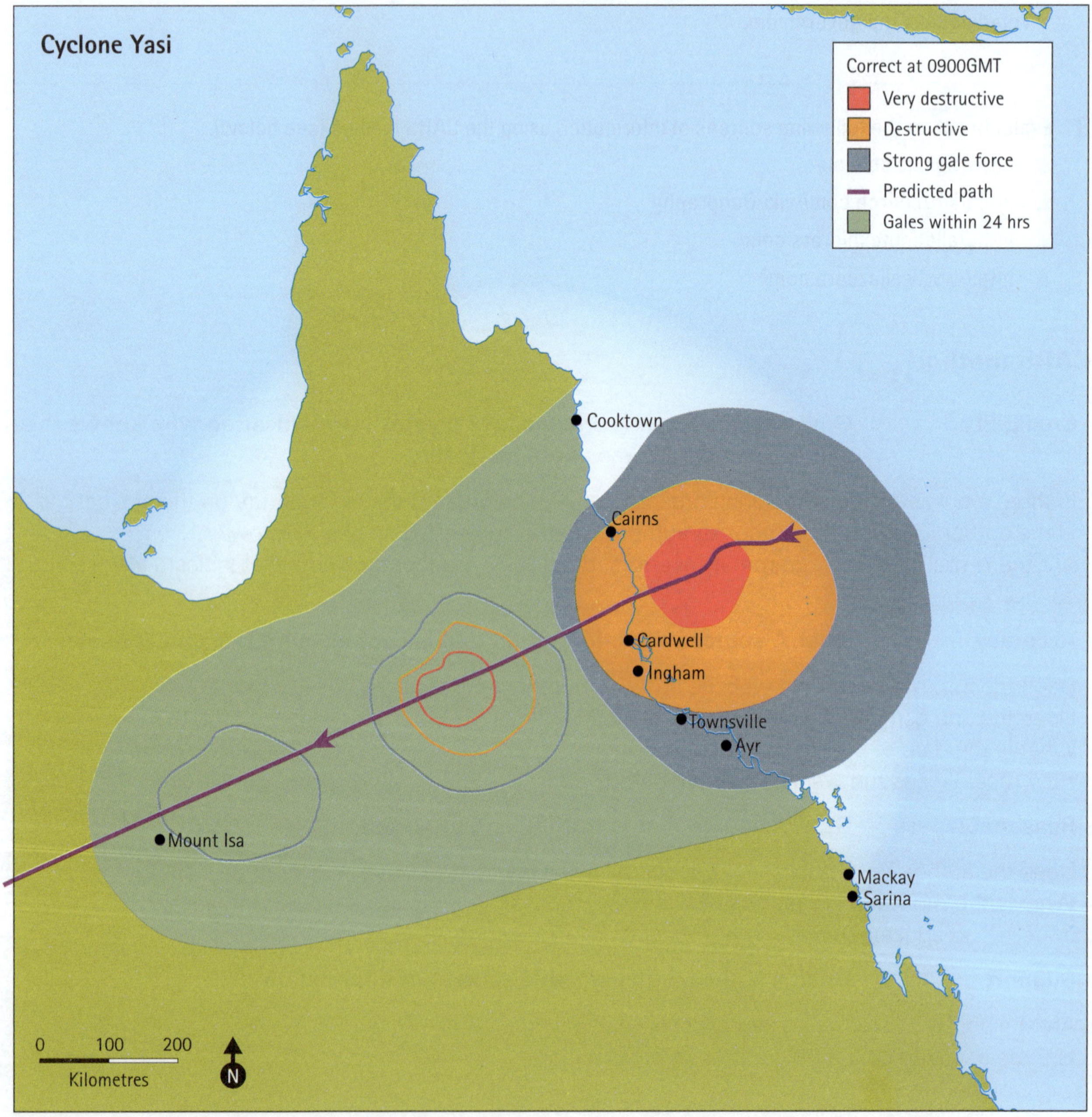

Source: MapsofWorld.com, with permission.

2 **a** Label the BOLTSS features on the map above.

b In which direction did Cyclone Yasi travel?

c Draw the symbol that would be used to show Cyclone Yasi on a weather map.

 ISBN 9780170367073

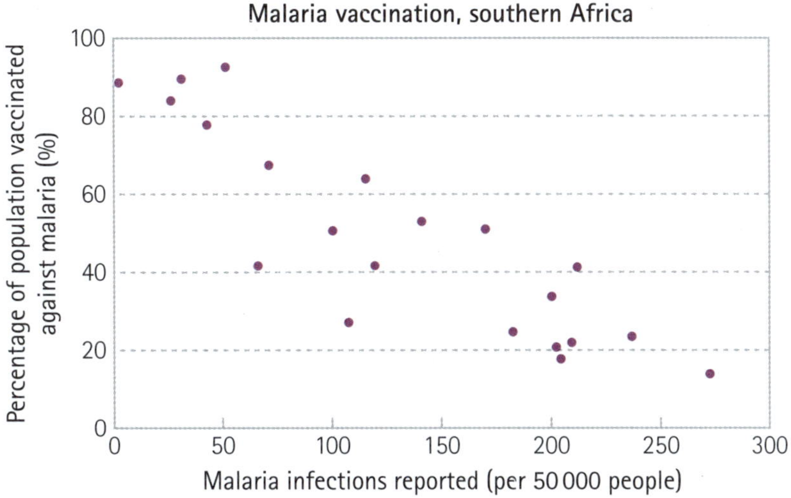

3 **a** The type of graph shown above is a ______________________ graph.

b The *x*-axis shows the ______________________.

c The *y*-axis shows the ______________________.

d The relationship shows that as ______________________ increases ______________________ decrease.

e Draw the line of best fit for this graph.

4 Tick (for true) or cross (for false) the following statements about latitude and longitude.

All lines of latitude are parallel	
All lines of longitude cross at the poles	
The 0 line of longitude is the Equator	
Lines of latitude are all the same length	
The Tropic of Cancer is a line of latitude	

5 Circle the correct answer for the following questions.

a $\frac{1}{5}$ = 20% / 24% / 30%

b Precis means explanation / summary / expansion.

c A percentage bar graph adds up to 1% / 10% / 100%.

d The layer of gases around the earth is the barometer / atmosphere / millibar.

e Lines on a weather map are called forecasts / gauges / isobars.

f A broken line on a weather map shows a trough / isobar / anticyclone.

g A stationary front means no air movement / fast wind / slow wind.

h The structure of a population is shown in a population pyramid / populi / slope.

i Inputs, outputs and processes are parts of a system / spiral / sag.

j Events repeated in a regular order make a cycle / flow / resource.

k Data in a group design is a linear / clustered / dispersed pattern.

ISBN 9780170367073

Answers

Unit 2

1 Asylum seekers – international; Salinity in the Murray-Darling Basin – national; School introduces new uniform – local; Climate change – global
2 Biosphere – crocodile, wattle, Great Barrier Reef; Lithosphere – earthquake, Mount Kosciuszko, gold; Hydrosphere – rain, flood, Sydney Harbour; Atmosphere – tornado, drought, ozone layer.

Unit 3

1 a i China
ii North-east of Chongqing, North-west of Yichang
iii 30° 49' N 111° 0'E
b Lots of steep hills and valleys and a little flatter where the dam has been placed
c 2 million people had to be moved to build the dam; it will provide power for people's homes
d In 1987 the river was a similar width all the way along and had smaller tributaries running into it. In 2006 the section upstream of the dam is much wider, including the tributaries. The area where the dam is located is three times wider than it was. The river downstream of the dam is the same width as it was before
e Flood the land, change the flow of the river, loss of silt further down the river, interrupt migration of fish
f Water is always available and produces as much power as 15 nuclear power stations; Does not produce CO_2
e National

Unit 4

1 a 25%
b 67%
c 20%
d 60%
2 a ACT
b Tasmania
c South Australia
d Victoria
e Northern Territory
f Western Australia
g Queensland
h New South Wales
Total: 100%
3 0–14: 36%; 15–64: 60%; 65+: 4%

Unit 5

1 a Australian Bureau of Statistics
b *y*-axis
c *y*-axis (vertical axis)
d *x*-axis
e *x*-axis (horizontal axis)
2 a x
b y
c 37%, African American women, USA
d 8%, women, France

Unit 6

1 a 65%
b English should take up the first seven squares and 7/10 of the eighth square
c Christianity should take up the first six squares of the graph and 1/10 of the seventh square

Unit 7

2 a Javanese
b Other
c Sundanese
d Madurese
e Coastal Malays
3 a 25–34
b 55 and over

Unit 8

1 a rapid increase
b fluctuating
c slow decrease
d rapid decrease then stable
e stable then rapid increase
2 a Urbanisation rates 2003–2013
b *x*-axis
c slow increase in change in urbanisation rate
d Indonesia
e 2007

Unit 9

1 a Negative
b None
c Positive
2 a Life expectancy versus total fertility rate in selected countries
b Life expectancy
c Total fertility rate
d 3
e negative
f increase
g Swaziland

Unit 10

1 a temperature
b rainfall
c mm
d °C
e 25 °C in January
f 11 °C in July
g 125 mm in April
h 75 mm in September
3 a millimetres (mm)
b degrees Celsius (°C)
c June, July, August
d average

Unit 11

1 a y; x
b male; female
c 15–64; 0–14; 65–85+
2 a 11.5 million
b 4.9 million
c 1.5 million
d 5–9

Unit 12

2 a four
b high, high, low, basic
c falling, low-slightly increasing, low-negative, new and emerging

ISBN 9780170367073

3 a three
  b four
  c two

Unit 14

2 a NE
  b N
  c SE

3 a west
  b south
  c east
  d south-west
  e north-east
  f north-west

4 a Border, Legend, Title, Scale, Source
  b north
  c west
  d north-east
  e south-west

Unit 15

1 a line scale
  b ratio: 1:25 000 000; words: One centimetre represents two hundred and fifty kilometres

2 Hyderabad

Unit 16

2 a tick
  b cross
  c cross
  d tick
  e tick

Unit 17

1 a high pressure
  b low pressure
  c isobars
  d north-west Tasmania, south-west Victoria, Brisbane, far north Queensland, south-west Western Australia
  e 4 hectopascals or millibars
  f hectopascals or millibars
  g cold and warm
  h occluded front and stationary front

2 a fine
  b slow breeze
  c a trough
  d close together

Unit 18

1 a volcano, Indonesia
  b ferris wheel, Germany
  c The Alton Barnes White Horse, England

2 a latitude
  b longitude
  c 40° S
  d Lord Howe Island
  e Tropic of Capricorn

Unit 19

Area reference for Area B is 03 14
Point D is 015 145

1 a 25 56
  b 28 52
  c 27 55

2 a historic monument
  b tennis centre
  c beacon
  d heliport
  e solar panels
  f cemetery
  g cool storage sheds
  h airstrip
  i berry gardens

Unit 20

1 a 250 m
  b 200 m
  c 150 m
  d 100 m
  e 50 m
  f 250 m

2 a depression
  b hill
  c ridge

3 a e.g. North Shire, Strathfield, Lockes Farm, Ryan Farm, A107, A5045
  b e.g. forest, lake, river, sea, wood
  c blue
  d contour lines
  e not steep

Unit 21

1 a valley
  b plateau
  c hill
  d plain

Unit 22

1 Human features: streets, water tower, causeway, bridge, reservoir, water supply installation, airport, cemetery, port, golf course, hospital, Natural features: beach, bay, reef, sea, creek, mangroves

2 a swamp
  b e.g. Mackay, racecourse
  c e.g. forest, Flat Top Island, Slade Islet
  d walking path
  e the width of the railway line
  f yes – the area is flat and close to river and ocean and there are already swamp areas outlined on the map
  g north-west
  h south
  i 1.3 km
  j 3.75 km
  k 29 68
  l 24 59
  m Flat Top Island; golf course; showground
  n 295 631; 234 598; 227 572

Unit 23

3 a title missing
  b border should be ruled
  c north point/orientation missing
  d legend missing
  e scale missing

Unit 26

1 a clustered, e.g. near a regional town
  b linear, e.g. along a river
  c linear, e.g. along a coastline

ISBN 9780170367073

3 a the world's major earthquakes
b linear
c e.g. around the 'Ring of Fire', along the west coast of North and South America and through the Asia–Pacific region.
d e.g. through Africa or the middle of the Pacific Ocean
e New Zealand

Unit 27

2

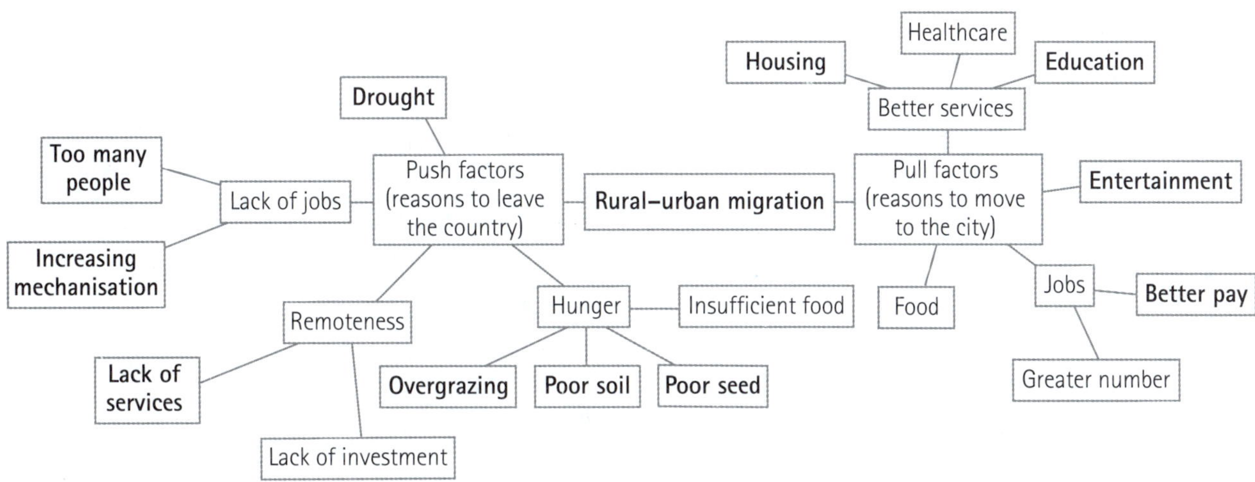

3 e.g. public transport

5

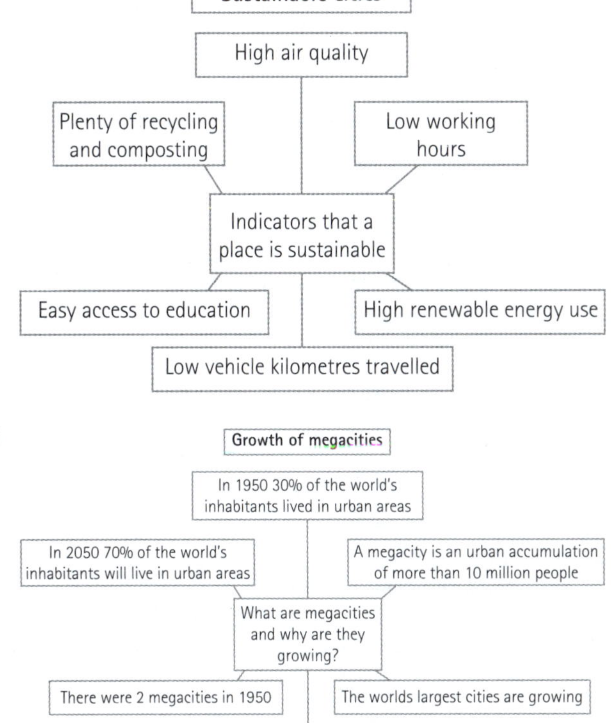

6

Unit 28

1 (First circle) Volcanic eruption (heading): Lava, ash and gases released; Magma pushed to the surface through a weakness in the Earth's crust
(Second circle) Earthquake (heading): Violent movements of earth's crust; Sends out shock waves
(Intersection of circles): Can kill people; Extreme natural event; Caused by plate movement in the Earth's crust

Unit 29

1 **Inputs**
solar energy
rainfall
bedrock

Processes
decay
plant decay
evapotranspiration
leaching
photosynthesis

Outputs
oxygen
through flow

Feedback
seeds
ground water
water

Unit 30

1 (L–R) condensation, precipitation, transpiration, run-off, percolation
2 In order starting from the top of the cycle: collection, processing centre, cleaners and screens, washing, forming, marketplace, community

Unit 31

1 In order: Warnings are given out to people; the tropical cyclone arrives; the Defence Force gives help straight away; Crops are replanted
2 In order: All bark and branches are removed and left at the coupe; After being trimmed and graded, logs are loaded onto trucks and sent to the saw mill; Logs are watered by sprinklers to prevent cracking and splitting; The best timber is left to dry for another 12 months and then kiln-dried for 7 days; Logs are broken down by a bandsaw to maximise profit

Unit 32

2 a Nicholson
  b Australian flag
  c politicians, experts and the media
  d El Niño
  e evaporation, condensation, precipitation
  f farmers and people in rural areas
  g so they can cope with the drought conditions
  h El Niño, drought, politics, farming, subsidies, water

Unit 33

1 a iii (968 000 km^2)
  b ii (1990)
  c i (December)
3 a cross
  b tick
  c tick
  d tick
  e cross

Unit 34

1
  1 tick
  2 cross
  3 tick
  4 cross
  5 tick
  6 cross
  7 tick
  8 tick
  9 cross
  10 cross
  11 tick
  12 cross
2 a national/regional/international
  b local
  c global
  d regional/international
  e national/international

Unit 35

1 Aquasure
2 State and federal governments
3 Local contractors
4 Local community
5 The Greens
6 Watershed Victoria

Unit 36

1 **Buildings:** Shops for lease, banks, chemist, petrol station, post office, supermarkets, restaurants, school
  Natural features: Trees on nature strip, lake, park
  Transport: Train station, lots of parked cars
  People: Pedestrians
  Tourist features: Playground, restaurants, park
  Management: Footpath, car parks on street, parking areas, 40-km zone, seating, speed humps, traffic lights, pedestrian lights, streets
  Developments: new apartment building

Unit 40

1 a O
  b F
  c O
  d F
  e O
  f F
  g F
  h F
2 a F
  b O
  c F
  d F
  e O
  f O
  g F
  h F
  i O
3 a 'This would mean that governments could have enough time to shut down essential services before they are damaged'
  b Research has been improved in the area of monitoring of seismic waves; it is likely that up to 30 seconds warning can be given to people

Unit 41

1 a Generalisation
  b Explanation
  c Example
  d Diagram
2 a i
  b ii
3 Students should choose paragraphs c (Generalisation), d (Explanation), e (Example) and f (Diagram).

Unit 42

1 a world wide web
  b search engine
  c company
2 a Japan aging population
  b Family planning India

Unit 43

1 **S**pace, **P**lace, **I**nterconnection, **C**hange, **E**nvironment, **S**ustainability, **S**cale
2 b south-west
  c

TC

3 a scatter
  b malaria infections reported
  c percentage of population vaccinated against malaria
  d malaria vaccination; malaria infections
4 tick; tick; cross; cross; tick
5 a 20%
  b summary
  c 100%
  d atmosphere
  e isobars
  f trough
  g no air movement
  h population pyramid
  i system
  j cycle
  k clustered

ISBN 9780170367073